////

"In sharp pieces infused with a yearning for decolonized love and freedom, Belcourt, of the Driftpile Cree Nation, ably balances poetic, philosophical, and political insights throughout this unique book... An urgently needed, unyielding book of theoretical and intimate strength."
—*KIRKUS REVIEWS*, **STARRED REVIEW**

"At just 23 years old, Belcourt won the Griffin Prize for Poetry for his book *This Wound Is a World*—he's also been a Rhodes scholar and, now, is publishing his first book of prose, a memoir that begins with his early life in Joussard, Alta, on the Driftpile First Nation and goes on to explore loves, sexual exploration and intimacy."
—**DEBORAH DUNDAS**, *TORONTO STAR* **"TWENTY BOOKS YOU NEED TO KNOW ABOUT IN SPRING 2020"**

"Wow. This book completely blew me away. I finished it and started right back in to pick at the nuanced and knotted language that emits from Belcourt. This is a phenomenal exploration of the poetics of queerdom and isolation and loneliness as philosophy, and as a collection of essays it stands alone. It exists as a statement of pure joy while at the same time delves deep into the (thoroughly complicated and corrupted) self. I can't wait to share this with everyone I know, I see Billy-Ray going far."
—**RYAN EVANS**, **WORD BOOKSTORE**

"*A History of My Brief Body* is a storm raging at the crossroads of post-structuralist, decolonial, and queer theory. Here, is a catalog of the abuses levied against brown and queer bodies by a monolith of past and present. Here, also, is a litany towards the unmaking of these abusive structures. Billy-Ray Belcourt commands a sophisticated range of politics and philosophy, presented here with prose as brutal in truth as it is beautiful in form. The result is a moving swirl of personal artifacts, salvaged from and brought to bear against a persistent, callous history in the pursuit of a compassionate, emancipated future."
—CONNOR MASON, THE BOOK LOFT

"These essays transcend genre and become something else entirely—a poetic masterpiece of self love and becoming. Billy-Ray Belcourt is one of the best we've got."
—GARY LOVELY, THE BOOK LOFT

"Billy-Ray Belcourt exposes colonialism's historical and ongoing brutality against both the North American Indigenous and queer experiences. Through theory, memoir, and poetry, Belcourt notates an 'archive of injuries' to then shape joy beyond known parameters. These essays are a glorious way to be held accountable. Bill-Ray Belcourt writes for his body, his being; read for yours."
—HEIDI BIRCHLER, MOON PALACE BOOKS

"I choose not to reduce *A History of My Brief Body* to simply a bending of genre. Well beyond that simple idea, Billy-Ray Belcourt uses a dexterity of language and form as a container

for memory and nostalgia as vehicles for truth about a still-blooming present. I love a book where a writer treats themselves and their own histories with gentleness and care, and this book is a towering achievement on that front."
—HANIF ABDURRAQIB, AUTHOR OF *THEY CAN'T KILL US UNTIL THEY KILL US, GO AHEAD IN THE RAIN,* AND *A FORTUNE FOR YOUR DISASTER*

"Billy-Ray Belcourt's moving and important book *A History of My Brief Body* dazzles in its quest to prove 'Joy is art is an ethics of resistance.' Not quite memoir, not quite poetry, not quite novel, this dizzying and intelligent book traces a queer NDN coming-of-age with equal parts search and insight. The book draws inspiration from the likes of Claudia Rankine, Terese Marie Mailhot, and Maggie Nelson, but Belcourt is no mimic; with *A History of My Brief Body*, Belcourt takes his place among these important thinkers."
—DANNY CAINE, RAVEN BOOK STORE

"In *A History of My Brief Body*, Billy-Ray breaks apart the reflection of a life into the specificity of moments—both his own and our collective experience—and beads them into his simultaneously sharp and lush writing. Bursting with all the movements of sex, riot, and repose, this book presents us with a shock of recognition and reclamation, and we are better for it—punch drunk and aching but, oh, so much better. I'm gutted by his brilliant mind."
—CHERIE DIMALINE, AUTHOR OF *EMPIRE OF WILD* AND *THE MARROW THIEVES*

"Settler colonialism demands we believe we'd be better off without our bodies—their needs, their feelings, their raucous disobedience and ungovernable change. I don't always know how to talk back to the violent nonsense that says, *Disappear.* With precision and care, Billy-Ray Belcourt presses thought against feeling to make, in each essay, an unbounded space for knowing and for staying whole."
—**ELISSA WASHUTA, AUTHOR OF *MY BODY IS A BOOK OF RULES***

"*A History of My Brief Body* puts the reader at the center of a deeply serious struggle—with language, with sexuality, with race and colonial Canada, and with love and joy and a life in art. It's about the attempt to stand in a center one has created, all while feeling the impossibility of ever doing so, and also wondering if maybe one shouldn't. This is a passionate and vital autobiography about the intellect, the culture, and the flesh, as it bears its assaults and preserves a true light."
—**SHEILA HETI, AUTHOR OF *MOTHERHOOD* AND *HOW SHOULD A PERSON BE?***

Also by Billy-Ray Belcourt

This Wound Is a World
NDN Coping Mechanisms: Notes from the Field

A HISTORY OF
MY BRIEF BODY

Billy-Ray Belcourt

Two Dollar Radio
Books too loud to Ignore

Two Dollar Radio
Books too loud to ignore

WHO WE ARE TWO DOLLAR RADIO is a family-run outfit dedicated to reaffirming the cultural and artistic spirit of the publishing industry. We aim to do this by presenting bold works of literary merit, each book, individually and collectively, providing a sonic progression that we believe to be too loud to ignore.

TwoDollarRadio.com

Proudly based in
Columbus
OHIO

@TwoDollarRadio

@TwoDollarRadio

/TwoDollarRadio

SOME RECOMMENDED LOCATIONS FOR READING *A HISTORY OF MY BRIEF BODY*: at your kokum's house, in a political science lecture, in a bed next to a Grindr hookup, or pretty much anywhere because books are portable and the perfect technology!

AUTHOR PHOTO→
Tenille Campbell

COVER PHOTO→

Valentin Ottone, *Running*, Sep. 11, 2009, flickr.com/photos/saneboy/3910861938

An earlier version of "Fatal Naming Rituals" was published in *Hazlitt* in 2018. "Notes from an Archive of Injuries" was published in the Winter 2020 issue of *Prairie Fire*.

To those for whom utopia is a rallying call

Author's Note

If I were to rank my aesthetic concerns, ambiguity would come before veracity. As such, some names and identifying features have been altered. What's more, I marshal the forces of poetry and theory to weave not a linear story, which "memoir" typically denotes, but rather a series of stories and analytical scenes into a composite that exceeds the boundaries of my individual life.

Failure to hear will matter to those who do not listen and those who are not heard, not only because stories without an audience do not survive but also because being heard or ignored impacts how the past resonates in the present.
—Jill Stauffer, *Ethical Loneliness: The Injustice of Not Being Heard*

I am not interested in longing to live in a world in which I already live.
—Maggie Nelson, *Bluets*

CONTENTS

Preface: A Letter to Nôhkom 3

Introduction: A Short Theoretical Note 7

An NDN Boyhood 11

A History of My Brief Body...23

Futuromania...33

Gay: 8 Scenes 49

Loneliness in the Age of Grindr 59

Fragments from a Half-Existence 67

An Alphabet of Longing 79

Robert 89

Notes from an Archive of Injuries.......................................99

Please Keep Loving: Reflections on Unlivability 103

Fatal Naming Rituals 113

To Hang Our Grief Up to Dry...119

Acknowledgments...131

Notes..133

A HISTORY OF MY BRIEF BODY

PREFACE: A LETTER TO NÔHKOM

This isn't a book about you, nôhkom. A book about you, a book in which you appear uncomplicatedly in a world of your own making, is an anti-nation undertaking. Canada is in the way of that book. To write that book I would need to write crookedly and while on the run. I would need to write my way out of a map and onto the land. For now, you move in and out of my books as though wind in a photograph. I swear no one will mistake you for a deflated balloon hanging from my fist. Here, and in my poetry, you're always looking up at the sky, longing for the future. In order to remember you as a practitioner of the utopian, I need to honor the intimacies of the unwritten. This book, then, is as much an ode to you as it is to the world-to-come. In the world-to-come, your voice reminds those in your orbit that we can stop running, that we've already stopped running.

Often I remember that you likewise have been denied the relief and pleasure of stillness. When I do, my heart breaks. When it does, I gather the shards into the shape of a country, then I close my eyes and swallow.

/////

Courtney, my oldest sister, and I have a running joke about how you call her only when you're searching for me, because for whatever reason you can't find me between the hundreds or thousands of kilometers that make the world too wide for you to be beside me anymore. In the summer of 2016, for example,

I traveled to Honolulu for the gathering of the Native American and Indigenous Studies Association. Before I boarded the plane you said this to me over the phone: "Don't forget to call me, because I'll go crazy if I don't hear from you."

What a sentence! Built into the mechanics of love is the possibility of mismanagement, for we can never adequately anticipate how our relation to a love object might shift or morph over time. Love has a tendency to shatter; it is prone to weakening and to running amok without notice. Perhaps, ironically, this is how it anchors us to a world, how it makes us want to give everything to the project of living well with others. Without love or the object into which we hoard parts of ourselves, we might go "crazy," lose our bearings. Although distance and time have pried open a barely translatable gap between you and me, we still find something worth tending to in the history of us that is unavailable elsewhere.

You love to tell the story about how when Jesse, my twin brother, and I were babies, you had to sit me in a jumper and him in a saucer to feed us concurrently. You would shovel a bit of oatmeal into my mouth, then turn to Jesse, you inform us, smirking. You fill the room with laughter each time you describe and re-enact how impatiently I would wait for my helping. Begging, high energy—you had to pick up the pace to appease me. I'm floored, not only by your ability to call up a decades-old memory, but also and more acutely by the joy that having had such an experience brings you.

Even in my earliest memories, I've always intuited your presence as a capacious one. I was a "kokum's boy," so to speak. You took me everywhere—albeit not to the bingo hall! You showed me a level of unconditional love that I rarely find at all nowadays. You were and are at the core of an extended family unit, balancing, back then, the fine line of encounter between my mom and my dad, your relatives and his. As kids, as you know all too well, Jesse and I rarely spent the night anywhere but our little house in the bush. Yes, we often made ambitious plans to do otherwise, but you always answered our late-night phone calls spurred by a sudden bout of sickness and then drove anywhere between fifteen to thirty minutes to fetch us. Truth be told, we were seldom ill; we simply wanted to be where you were.

It seems now that this flow of emotion has inverted as I've grown up. Today, I sometimes forget to call when I said I would, or I habitually wait for your number to flash across my phone. This monumental change is a disorienting fact of adult life—we stretch outside the collective skin of the family. But back then your love incubated a refuge, one I can always return to if need be.

To speak of the possibility of losing me because I'm not near you might also point to the ways that we inhabit imperiled bodies in a shrinking world in which we don't remember how to coexist without stymying collective flourishing. It's as though you're saying, à la Warsan Shire, that I'm "terrifying and strange and beautiful, someone not everyone knows how to love."[1] It's as though you're warning me that your house might be the only sanctuary for NDN boys who love at the speed of utopia.

Nôhkom, I'm not safe. Canada is still in the business of gunning down NDNs. What's more, state violence commonly manifests as a short-circuited life, one marked by illness, sadness, and other negative affects by which we become ruled until what remains of a body is more so a ghoulish trace. Despite the stories of progress and equality at the core of Canada's national identity, a long tradition of brutality and negligence is what constitutes kinship for the citizens of a nation sat atop the lands of older, more storied ones. I can't promise I won't become snared in someone's lethal mythology of race. What I can do is love as though it will rupture the singularity of Canadian cruelty (irrespective of whether this is a sociological possibility). Herein lies my poetic truth.

Love, then, isn't remotely about what we might lose when it inevitably dissipates. How unworkable love would be were we to subject it to a risk-cost benefits analysis! In the world of the statistical it doesn't survive and is stripped of its magic; love dwells somewhere less rhythmed by anticipation, less mediated by prediction and calculation, all of which fools us into fighting to preserve a sovereignty that doesn't exist. In *Cruising Utopia: The Then and There of Queer Futurity*, José Esteban Muñoz writes: "To accept the way in which one is lost is to be also found and not found."[2] What has stayed constant between us is this cycle of losing and finding, this unending transference of vitality, without which we might feel directionless. Love of this sort, however, isn't about making a roadmap to an other who then becomes your compass. It is a proposition to nest in the unrepayable and ever-mounting debt of care that stands in opposition to the careless and transactional practices of state power that mire the lives of NDNs and other minoritized populations. Having inherited your philosophy of love, which is also a theory of freedom, nôhkom, I can write myself into a narrative of joy that troubles the horrid fiction of race that stalks me as it does you and our kin.

It's likely that you might feel confused at times by my style of writing, its dexterity, its refusal of easiness, but I know that you'll sense the affection bubbling up inside each word. That affection is joy, and it started with you. Now, I see it everywhere.

kisahkihitin,
Bill, Edmonton, AB

INTRODUCTION: A SHORT THEORETICAL NOTE

I wear worn-out words everywhere I go. In the museum of political depression[1], which is the world-at-large, I'm routinely mistaken for an item in an exhibition about the havoc of modernity, for I'm always out of step with the clock of the historical. As an NDN, this hiccup, this moment of amnesia, isn't new to me. Words stick to me like a loner to the sight of nothingness. I shape-shift between the position of the loner and the sight of nothingness. In either role, I stockpile letters, all bloated with symbolic power, for they are the products of a history that isn't done with the discursive. With rebellion in mind, I aim them at a tomorrow free from the rhetorical trickery of colonizers everywhere. The alphabet, grammar, and syntax—these are my mass-produced emotional cargo. My body is the vehicle for transport, which means my heart is an engine. This aspect of my embodiment shadows me like an open secret. With which concepts, then, might we instruct one another how to be more *here* than we already are? To allow others to comprehend that we are deserving of and that we already practice this expansive here-ness?

In the museum of political depression, in its tidied halls, books of the sort I want to write are banned, for they are against the world that birthed the writer. Books that emerge from a banned way of thinking, that pry open space to live otherwise in an uninhabitable world, lie open in hospitals and university dorms and community libraries but rarely in an institution governed by a pessimism of the future and a romance of the present. I'm both native to and an exile in a museum where hope disappears in clouds of misery. Quickly, I learned to walk upside down on the ceiling of the museum, which is an artistic practice of sorts. That is how I wrote this book. From this point of view, I could spot breaks in the clouds everywhere.

What I try to do in what follows is shore up another kind of emotional atmosphere, one in which the museum as that which governs NDN life, that makes our bodies into vessels for a vengeful past and nothing else, is emptied of its political wrath. I call this ecology of feeling, this anti-institutional world, joy. I could call it a number of positive feelings—happiness, exuberance, wonder—but with joy I want to bring into focus a durational performance of emotion, one that is caught up in an ancestral art of world-making in the most asphyxiating of conditions. Joy by and for the racialized is what we can consider the practice of breathing in what theorist Christina Sharpe calls "breathtaking spaces" shaped by oppressive forces of all kinds.[2] How do a people who have been subject to some of the country's most programmatic and legal forms of oppression continue to gather on the side of life? Under what furtive conditions do they enact care against the embargo on care that is Canada?

Wherever there's an injunction on something as integral to the livability of the world as joy, there is underground activity, a fugitive cooperative of feeling, a commune of love that isn't to be perceived by the dominant eye. In this book, I track that un-Canadian and otherworldly activity, that desire to love at all costs, by way of the theoretical site that is my personal history and the world as it presents itself to me with bloodied hands. To my mind, joy is a constitutive part of the emotional rhetoric and comportment of those against whom the present swells at an annihilating pace. With joy, we breach the haze of suffering that denies us creativity and literature. Joy is art is an ethics of resistance.

To provide an account of the ways in which NDNs enact a form of geographic escape that is still unfolding, we need to write against the unwritability of utopia. This means that joy is somewhat of an impossible desire when our sorrow is multiplied as long as daily life continues unimpeded. That we experience joy, however, that we can identify it, if only belatedly, illuminates the dead end toward which the settler state hurls. In our insistence against elimination, the logical holes in the fabric of a colonial world are revealed. Wherever light rushes in is an exit route.

These pages don't eschew sadness and sorrow; in fact, many of them traffic in those hard feelings. I have to tell my story properly, and to do this I need to guide you through a cacophony of things that could break a heart without negating the sociological import of our enactments of care. I'm up against decades and perhaps centuries of a literary history that extracted from our declarations of pain evidence of our inability to locate joy at the center of our desire to exist. With you, I can rally against this parasitic way of reading, this time-worn liberal sensibility. Together we can detonate the glass walls of Canadian habit that entrap us all in compressed forms of subjectivity.

Join me in the ruins of the museum of political depression! With hints of a world-to-come everywhere we are and have been, a red utopia is on the horizon!

AN NDN BOYHOOD

My twin brother, Jesse, and I were born marked by a history of colonization and a public discourse of race we can't peel from our skin. We were made to take on a mode of embodiment that erodes from the inside out with vicious precision. At the same time, we came into being because love is mathematical: when two people desire each other, they multiply, in various shapes and forms. In our very corporeality we are thus a container for the terror of the past and the beauty that it can't in the end negate. In this way we, like NDN boys everywhere, are subliminal.

The first year of Jesse's and my life was a hotbed of decisions, desires, and disavowals that would hover above our shared emotional worlds deep into adolescence. This isn't my story to tell in painful and careful detail, so the picture I paint now is one that's rehashed from a handful of sources, including something like intuition.

Here goes. My mom and dad loved while coated in the ash of history. Twenty-somethings entranced by the ecstasy of optimism, they made a family out of nothing but the human need to be a part of something less resonant with toxicity than solitude. They didn't know how to ask the question Sheila Heti poses in *Motherhood*: "Who is it for me to bring all this unfolding into being?"[1] Perhaps the philosophical basis for their children's lives was that they no longer wanted to exhale smoke.

////

If we subscribe to the idea that we inherit bits and pieces of the psychosocial habits of our family, then my parents' approach to life-making might also be descriptive of mine today, in their aftermath. Perhaps this pressurized orientation to memory—one by which we understand the past as a trace that pulsates in a body in the present—is always the case with life-writing. The writer is called on by others to do the politically significant and ethically charged work of construction and then documentation. This is my job: to report from the scene of an undead past colliding with a still-to-be-determined future.

////

By the age of twenty-three, my mom had four children, two girls and two boys, between the ages of three months and five years. My dad says Jesse (his legal name is Jesse-Lee) and I were named so as to usher us into the world of rodeo. I've seen the pictures of toddler-me dressed up as a cowboy, my dad positioned in the corner of the frame, smiling, perhaps bathing in the scene of self-recognition before him. Names are worldly, and it was with that knowledge, that emotional and maternal knowledge, that my mom gave us her last name, passed on to her from her dad. I imagine this was a rare practice in the nineties in northern Alberta, which was unshakably conservative. I like to think my mom did this to foreground our enmeshment, how irrevocably *hers* we are, how even outside of the womb we populate the affective house of her, then and now.

The story goes, my mom and dad fell out of love, hard, with an always-accelerating speed, shortly after our birth. A forest fire can't be a refuge. My mom wanted to live in a land without a dangerous weather—in this way, we're profoundly alike. According to my dad, he went about the drama of raising twins on the reserve, enlisting the aid of a similarly inexperienced nephew. Six months slowly inched by as his sense of maternality disintegrated. On our first birthday, having lived twelve months in an ecology of complicated love, of sociological forces that elided our awareness, we went under the care of my mom's mom, nôhkom. It's impossible to deny that this reorganization indelibly ordered Jesse's and my future, those collectively and individually lost and those newly birthed. Language is inadequate here to bring into focus the communal effort, involving an extended family unit that included my parents and their parents, that went into raising two NDN boys not in a way that would ignore the coloniality of the world but so as to engender life that might breach its grip. This is the old art of parenting in order to keep NDN kids safe from what lingers of a governmentally sanctioned death wish against them.[2]

////

NDN boys are ideas before they are bodied. Our lives are muffled by a flurry of accusations that outrun us.[3] Ideas of this vexed sort leave a burnt path in their wake. Feet like ours are singed with a history that isn't done with us. There is a point—call it a turning point—at which NDN boys can become angry men of at least two types (I'm not suggesting that this is fatalistic; the norms of gender and race fail to regulate us completely, to paraphrase Judith Butler): one that is imprisoning and riotous at once, a mode of being that sucks the air out of the room, and another that is quieter but equally denigrating, a slow injunction on happiness and possibility. Both beget a sense of immobility—these are ways of life at the heart of colonialism that cut along gendered lines. There is a host of violent acts done as a symptom of these performances of racialized masculinity. This is a well-documented facet of NDN life: the trauma of colonialism erupts in the minds and bodies of men, who then bombard the lives of women and girls, two-spirit peoples, and queers. Today, we are beholden to the work of feminist mothering and fathering to repair what has been done and to bring about boys and men who answer the call of democratizing the labor of care.

What is it to live, to suffer, and, above all, to love in an emotionally inflexible world fashioned to produce men who eat "too much of the sunset?"[4] We are haunted by that turning point, brought back to it again and again. But it doesn't once and for all consign us to a ravaged life. There is more to be said; there is another mode of life to inhabit.

////

In my first memory of nôhkom, she and I are on the couch in our home in the hamlet of Joussard, only a few kilometers from the place of our political and social belonging, Driftpile. What I remember most is a feeling of childish liveliness, which orbits nôhkom, and her enduring attentiveness to the ebb and flow of my behavior.

I've found myself unable to properly go about the task of articulating the infinitude of nôhkom's care. How does one thank another for manufacturing a world to experiment with the precarity of aliveness? I might spend the rest of my life inching closer to that place of articulation, to a place where her act of giving in to the demands of care are made visible, celebrated. How could I strive for anything but this unfinishable avowal? How does one remain unwaveringly answerable to this call from nowhere and everywhere? On the other hand, how do I resist enfleshing a writer-me that is obsessed with bringing into view this unrepayable debt while the world-me idles by? Too much can go missing in this space of translation. Maybe the onus isn't to sputter out in the ruts of the abstract, of the textual, but to live in a manner that cites those dear to the heart. Butler claimed that language and styles of behavior are citational, that they echo from a history of use. Joy, then, is a politics of citation.

////

Like most twins, Jesse and I were inseparable. We were Pokémon trainers and baseball players, boreal forest foragers and amateur engineers. At times, however, I strain to call up shared memories; I suspect this is because our senses of selfhood were intertwined, that we were bound up in a "you" and an "us" and a "we" that hardened into a singular entity over time, having begun in utero. What I do know is that many, relatives and otherwise, made us out to be opposites, good and bad, feminine and masculine, academic and unruly. Perhaps they were simply pointing out the parts of us that bifurcated, in opposition to our drive to enact a sameness that upset liberal norms of individuation. Maybe it's a mere psychosocial fact that the lives of twins are labyrinthine, like any other social form. There's a photograph of us from a Halloween in the late nineties; I'm dressed as Tinky Winky, the purple Teletubby, and Jesse is dressed as the blue Power Ranger. This artifact is regularly invoked as evidence of our disparate identities (and my nascent queerness). Nevertheless, Jesse and I were collaborators and accomplices, best friends and sometimes rivals. Which is to say that we too were key architects of the world of care that brought and is still bringing us into being, against the odds, in opposition to the insufficiencies of gender that colonialism yields.

////

"maybe i am here in the way that a memory is here? now, ain't that fucking sad and beautiful?"[5]

////

It is likely impossible to trace when, where, and under what conditions those who arrived with enmity on the shores of what is now improperly called Canada inaugurated a modality of gender that produced men who self-destruct. Surely a historian more disciplined than I has tried, but my suspicion is that one would end up again and again with an incomplete bag of events, theoretical inclinations, and emotional responses. That this blow to subjectivity doesn't invite curiosity from those outside our communities doesn't, however, lessen its cruelty and longevity. We might look to the testimonial record that burgeoned from the atrocities of the twentieth century bathed in the language of state care and fiduciary obligation. Here, for example, is the public testimony of a woman who was made to attend a residential school on Vancouver Island:

> I remember entering through the front doors,
> and the sound of those doors closing still
> haunts me when I go to places that look like
> . . . that building . . . when the door closes . . .
> The fear and the hurt . . . there's nothing you
> can do once you're . . . once you're there.[6]

Though not explicitly vocalized, we might hear in this harrowing account of the reverberations of the trauma of state education a nodal point in the history of colonization that has to do with the brutalization of NDNs at every conceivable level. This is to say that throughout the long twentieth century, Canada incubated death worlds where meaning was made to injure via the categories we have come to inhabit with ease. Part of what is ghoulish about the fungibility of those doors, those facades that lived on in horror-filled memories, is that they bear too the experience of gender as it was traumatically unmade and remade in the bodies of NDN children.

///

It's sometime in the early 2000s, and the wretchedness of history is still revealing itself, testimonial by testimonial, angered and shaken voice by angered and shaken voice, until there's a pileup of words and tears that Canada can't obliterate from its cultural memory. I can't identify the source of my curiosity, but I ask nimôsom if he'd been made to attend the Indian Residential School at Joussard. *Yes, but I don't want to talk about it,* he says without looking up from his plate.

This "Yes, but I don't want to talk about it" floats above our family like an open secret. I watch nimôsom struggle against emotion, against gender, but never waver in his drive to break from the spell of that haunted door, that omnipresent and cursed doorway, in order to provide for our family. Everywhere NDN men are in a struggle against gender.

///

There are cavernous gaps in my memory in which people I love with fortitude today, those without whom being in the world would be a taxing affair, don't exist, as though my brain has been surgically hampered. Rather than let those gaps swallow me up, I plant flowers of all sorts there. Daisies and prairie crocuses. Northern Alberta flowers that grow in the wild, ones that hold a firm place in my childhood psyche where bodies should be. There is no use marinating on the thorny question of how and for what reasons there is nothingness where there should be a haze of good feeling. A thick opacity is missing. Again, it isn't mine to estimate who or what was the thief in the prairie, subarctic night. Perhaps I write now, in the mode of autobiography, to stimulate the conditions that might call up that opacity, the fragile and engrossing density of memory. In this way, I'm an archaeologist of the disappeared.

///////

Nôhkom worked full-time as a receptionist at the health center on the reserve, so when nimôsom, a mechanic, had an uncompromising string of repairs to attend to at his garage, Jesse and I would stay at my dad's house, also on the reserve. In and out of his house flowed a host of relatives and family friends, all irrevocably thrown into the orbit of softness and openness that was my dad. To this day, his house is something of a brown commons, an ideational and affective infrastructure that, to use José Esteban Muñoz's language, "holds and shelters brown life within its walls,"[7] one that dissipates the governing power of the male property-bearer and proliferates space for other forms of life, other ways of togetherness. For the untutored eye, for the normatively socialized onlooker, my dad's house, his houses, might be best aestheticized as a disorderedness, one without law or social norm. It is, however, this anti-authoritarian rhythm that irradiates a more politically radical geography of care. In retrospect, this is likely why Jesse and I rarely wanted to leave when nôhkom came to retrieve us after work. This is what I want my home to make possible, the shelter for brown life I want to prop up, wherever I end up. This, then, is part of a feminist project that Maggie Nelson describes as a socialization or democratization of the maternal function, which is to ask: How are we to architect places through which NDN life flows, through which it isn't slowed down or disappeared but embraced and therefore multiplied?

////

I never felt the pressure to actualize my parents' dreams. Not one. Or, if any, it was the dream of making a life unhampered by the strictures of indecision and ignorance, which is probably something we all want for ourselves anyway. One time my dad said I was living the life that he could've had, had he refused to let anyone be the bearer of his optimism. I wonder what it is about my life now that he wishes for his past self, the self-that-could-have-been. Like most parents, he inspects me through the rosy filter of unconditional love, but he doesn't have enough material to develop a complex idea of the intricacies of Billy-Ray Belcourt the adult, who is different from Billy-Ray Belcourt the child. I don't mourn this lack of expectation, this absence of narcissism, which is the narcissism of wanting to see oneself in one's child, to have them bloom into another you. On the contrary, without a mirror held in front of me at all times, I felt without skepticism the platitude that anything was possible.

Maybe I spoke too soon. I remember the worrisome responses from a number of relatives upon the declaration of my queerness. Despite establishing in clear yet sparse wording that their happiness was contingent on my happiness, there was also a fog of grief. This was the grief of childlessness. In my vocalization of a non-normative sexual identity, they heard too a disavowal of futurity, that I had relocated permanently to a land emptied of fathers, one inhospitable to the customs of fatherhood. Perhaps in those seconds and minutes I became less like them, less *theirs*, less bound up in the ticking time bomb of social reproduction, so less beholden to the continuation of a name, a history. In the quiet variations of tone and tempo I heard the world rearrange in their minds. I watched their language ache and falter as I myself ached and faltered.

Regardless, I forgive them just as I forgive naive versions of myself. I choose instead to appreciate the vastness with which they think of my future self, however tied it is to a fiction over which I don't hold sovereignty. I can't blame my kin for forgetting that the form for my life's emotional content isn't, as one might expect, a family but an entire world, a wilderness ruled by unknowing inside which I'm a future relic. What binds us is the knowledge that it can be devastating to discover that a loved one has forfeited everything to that which you'll never fully see for yourself. To love someone is firstly to confess: *I'm prepared to be devastated by you.*

////

The noise of everyday life rings inside my head. This essay sits at the center of the multi-sensory labyrinth that is memory recall. When not distracted by other business, I, like a janitor, scan the darkened building of me for detritus and misplaced things, something to put me to work again. When nothing jolts me out of a stupor, I stare up at the ceiling, hoping something will drop onto my face, something with which to make a mess worth looking at, worth showing to others.

////

I didn't ever think I would write about this, but here we are. The conundrum is that the data that is the past isn't a block of clay we can, like an artist, press our hands into. Some of us might seek to be one step ahead of memory, to whittle the loose ends of our personal histories down to a single knowable object (a block of clay or a diary or a memoir), to expose a kind of hidden or suppressed truth, to give it a form, to contain it, to master it. It is difficult to discern when I'm doing this and when I'm not.

In my case, the memory is one I've let slip from my mouth only two times. Even now I won't divulge all the details. The first person with whom I had sex was a dear friend. He and

I spoke few words and no complete sentences. In the absence of language, we activated the textuality of gesture and emotion, of sense and sensation. This repeated in the thick of one hot summer. It matters what I call this now, so I hesitate to call it anything. Perhaps if it were a performance art piece I could call it *My Subjectivity* or *Becoming a Subject in the Shadow of Language* rather than having to make do with the tropes of the coming-of-age story. That this encounter has seldom lived in the world of speech, hasn't grown a skin of its own, perplexes me still. Memory, it seems, isn't always material out of which to make art. Sometimes remembering refuses us. Sometimes I'm a shoreline the water of memory drags its palm across.

////

It's August 2012. I give the valedictory address in a church behind the high school. In it, I spend a great deal of time thanking family and friends for their contributions to my upbringing, to my becoming-human. During the softly named "rose ceremony," I cry as I hug a number of my relatives. As the graduates empty out of the room, I hug my dad, who is sitting with his partner and their kids near the altar. I realize everyone is taking in the spectacle of two NDN men in a familial embrace, both of us overcome with emotion. In those piercing seconds, we were possibility more than anything else, a mode in which NDN men rarely exist. In hugging me, my dad teaches me how to hold. In hugging me, my dad teaches me how to be held.

At night, I turn down the lights with this image. It gives me a nocturnal language—something with which to go about the unglamorous work of survival.

A HISTORY OF MY BRIEF BODY

Let's start with the body, for so much is won and lost and lost and lost there.

////

I was lonely once and that was all it took. A thick haze, a smothering opacity, this was the loneliness of feeling estranged from one's body and, by extension, the world. My loneliness asked nothing of me; it festered with inattention. Rarely did it think out loud. I neglected my loneliness and it expanded with animosity. My loneliness grew into a forest atop me.

////

There are over seventeen million results when one googles *Is it possible to cry oneself to death?*

////

I was a haunted teenager, so much so that every photo of me also featured an apparition of sorts—an unseen and unseeable force-presence that, like a parasite, flourished in the wasteland of me. One of the first things I did when I moved out of nôhkom's house and to Edmonton to attend the University of Alberta was delete my first Facebook account. I self-abolished. I had lost fifty pounds since 12th grade and wanted to undergo a process of self-making that wasn't shadowed by a past-me.

At this funeral of me in a west-end hotel room, I made myself anew, destroying the photographic record of my adolescence. Now, it's difficult to find photographs of this time. In this way, I made waste out of history. What's more, I made myself exist less. I lost more weight, shrunk myself. I ate less and spoke quieter. I deflated everything I could. As such, I internalized the ugliness of colonialism. I pitted the world against myself. For years, I ate photo albums as late-night snacks. Most days I cowered before the mirror. Other days, dimmer ones, I placed a ban on my reflection; the ecstasy of not knowing was a buzz I rarely rebuffed.

////

To be queer and NDN is paradoxical in that one is born into a past to which he is also unintelligible. I wasn't born to love myself every day.

There is a dead future with my name on it in the territory of my people. There isn't much one can do but run when the future becomes roadkill. I didn't wish to find out what it might take to incorporate roadkill into the everyday, to drain it of shock value. One would likely need to sacrifice inner life, uninvent it. In Introduction to the History of Art, which I took years ago, the instructor informed us that photography, much like portraiture, enticed many to rethink the contours of the self, also sometimes called the soul. Perhaps in leaving I didn't choose to be soulless. I chose instead to continue looking at myself.

Is there anything left to say about the closeted gay kid? Sometimes I think, without pathos, that the coming-out story is endangered, and rightfully so. Best left in the previous century, where it teemed with subversiveness. Back then, to confess to desire in a different direction was to expose oneself to existential risk, among other types. The avowal—*you are gay*—had every-thing to do with a refusal of the world-as-it-was. (This calls to my mind Foucault's Beauvoirian insistence that homosexuality isn't what one *is* but what one *does*.) There need not be new narratives of this sort because they are already there, archived, fixed in the zeitgeist. Other days, I'm desperate for everyone to know that I sat, seasick, overcome by lightheadedness, in the closet, imagined and material, like all feral metaphors. I thought I was to drown. I drowned. *YOU'RE SPEAKING TO A MANNEQUIN*, I wanted to shout to everyone within earshot. I was arrested by my own tragic story. I took pity on myself. Édouard Louis: "I didn't want to carry a pain that I didn't choose."[1] I see it everywhere on the rez, when talking to men on Grindr—the aftereffects of surviving a struggle against oneself, against an identity you're squished inside. I didn't know what to do with my agony, so I did what most do with the at once unknown and menacing: I waged a war on it, on myself. Desire appeared around me as a flammable entity. I ran around with my hands on fire. I have died. I have lived. What glory!

Symptomatic of the loneliness of the closet was how devoted I became to the prospect that I would die at a young age. At thirteen or fourteen, I discovered a lump on my right testicle while masturbating. I already felt that I'd come into the world in a frenzy the way a volcano's eruption creates an archipelago. I believed that my longing was poisonous and thus I had begot the lump on my genitals; in a biblical fashion, my punishment was meted out on the body. I took a vow of silence. I lived terribly in a village of no one and nothing. I'll always have one foot there, in the wet, shimmering grass.

I didn't know where to go, but I knew I had to be in flight. I slipped out the bathroom window. No one was looking. No one knew how to look at me in those dying days. I went to what many in northern Alberta affectionately call "the City," Edmonton. I was non-existent, yet to come, and alive in a hypothetical tomorrow. I wished to assassinate history's version of me, put him to rest, let him soar into the clouds like a floating lantern. I wanted to be there, below him, with a single candle, crying for the last time.

As a teen, I devoured dystopian and queer novels to put to use the existential deferral that narrative elicits. Teens don't read for beauty, but to practice the art of disappearance. Today, I read and write for beauty, and live so as to disappear.

If I'm more of a toy to be wound up than a man, can I write beautiful things? What I mean is that I don't subscribe to the fantasy of self-sovereignty, knowing fully that the past starts into my brief body like a knife.[2] My hands are made up of a set of hands that puppeteer me. The hands aren't God's. They are History's. Its sores are mine.

The past came with me to Edmonton. It's like a layer of dust on everything, so granular it encases me.

I have found myself a number of times driving in the direction of the old apartment in which I spent many weekends with unlovable men out of neither nostalgia nor habit but a yearning for revenge. I believe it is a writer's job to tend to memory in its last hours, as though a nurse in an infirmary. Lately, however, I want to hunt memory, to sink my teeth into it, to transform it into a gangly creature I might terrorize. In undergrad I was taught that horror films enflesh worldly anxieties, enabling us to confront and thus banish them into the unreal, after which we return to "reality" with a non-violent disposition. This displacement of volatile emotion wasn't what I was after. I wanted to watch memory squirm. To torture it as it had me. I wanted it to lock eyes with me in a pale, trembling light.

The eyes of a man I sleep with are dead, like an empty street, always on the verge of mutinous activity. His face emits an explosive kind of impressionability, so much so that I suspect a man—any man—could get him to drop his underwear once more were he instructed accordingly, even though he has just orgasmed. Strangely, this makes me think of a special viewing of Barry Jenkins's *Moonlight* I attended in Oxford. The film hadn't been widely distributed in the UK outside of London, so the theatre was full of queer and black students, all of whom were there not passively to consume a film but to be bodiless for ninety minutes, to have the unbearability of their longing momentarily suspended or supplanted with another's. (This is also the closest I've come to a definition of love.) When the credits rolled, I realized that even though the film had gotten under my skin, ruptured it, eviscerated it, the experience of affection wasn't mine, wasn't private. Sometimes when I fuck, I fuck not in the name of futurity but as a symptom of a romance with the negative, a romance with my own injurability. Perhaps there is something queer to be said of the act of running around without a skin. Lee Edelman: "The queerness of which I speak would deliberately sever us from ourselves."[3]

Fucking won't rescue me from my longing.

This revelation came to me as though ventriloquized from a part of my consciousness hidden in the apartment. My hands sweat with it. Add this to the evidence that I'm innately and intricately fucked up.[4] A pop psychoanalyst (which is to say that I read a bit of Freud in undergrad and queers are melancholics writ large, so I speak with experiential authority), I suspect that this kind of indefatigable longing can be the origin of an artistic disposition. "Loneliness is a kind of dysphoria with the world" is a refrain that repeats in my body of writing. It's a hunch of mine that no one can apologize for or administer a cure for the racialized and sexualized condition of existential ennui. The sum of all political actors, of all the puppets of the state, can only render the apology an ever-engrossing work of fiction, an all-consuming atmosphere of white noise, something to which I would be bound against my will. Apologies for an engineered catastrophe, constrained by a fetishization of the present, threaten to pin me to reality, and I'm interested in something far more real. The cure isn't conjurable in government offices. It's a matter of time, of temporality. An anachronism, I've spent my youth in a tale of contradiction. My outsider status is the price I pay for a mode of attunement and perception that compels me to write into the airless grip of an unattainable object of desire. Utopia, of course, is an impossible love object. But as such, it is also an incitement to write, to run with pen in hand into the negative space of the future. Would I have it another way? What a danger to creativity, after all, to find oneself fitting neatly into the world!

If I'm a writer, it's because to be an NDN is to be a concept that speaks. I live in the world of ideas because it's the world of my people. If I'm a writer, it's because to be queer is to worship loss—and what is a book but a losing game?

Back to fucking. When I first downloaded Grindr in 2014, I wielded the app like a weapon in a war of emotion. I was a soldier slippery with regret. In each new bed, hungrier than the last, I surrendered so much. I surrendered with fevered surety. To and from each bedroom I went with my wounded shadow hanging over my shoulder.

One long summer night, I agreed to meet a man who refused to send a picture of his face. He told me he was handsome and white and that he had a nice dick. I'd slept with handsome white men with nice dicks in the past, so I could summon an image of him that titillated, that felt tangible and authentic. I also felt like I was taking part in a tradition of random sex between men for whom faces are secondary erotic materials—a gay rite of passage. I arrived at the Delta in downtown Edmonton, where he was staying, motored by the possibility of my impending death, which is perhaps one of our species' oldest aphrodisiacs; if not, surely this is the case for gay men. He met me in the lobby, as the elevators were keycard-operated. I fixated on his attire, which was outdated, possibly socioculturally or religiously mandated, or both. I felt a pang of pity, which mixed with fear and horniness to usher me into an altered state akin to jet lag or vertigo. I was losing self-control with each passing second. When he waved me inside the elevator, I complied without hesitation. His room was lit only by the pay-per-view gay porn on the TV. The porn was interracial, which was likely intentional, and this made me chuckle to myself. He was readying himself to fuck a symbol. Like a good symbol, I didn't speak. A creature of habit, I dutifully sucked his dick, which was heavily forested by pubic hair (the first clue that he was in a heterosexual marriage). Not wanting to cum prematurely, he lifted me up and sat me on the queen-sized bed, pushing me back with his left hand, which wasn't slowed down by the gold wedding band (the second clue), as one might hope. I knew that a tongue against a butthole could engender an earth-shattering sensation, but what I experienced was the tremor of how spoiled his desperation made me. While he tongued me I thought not of his wife but of my own impermanency. I went numb, for I had become a neighborhood through which the aggrieved and unlively pass idly, with their eyes closed. I was an iconography of erasure. Nonetheless, I felt useful as his tongue drilled into me. I wanted to give a man a song to sing. I wanted to begin where his mouth opened.

In James Baldwin's *Giovanni's Room*, Ellen, a motherly figure in the narrator's life, reminds her husband that "a man . . . is not the same thing as a bull." The connotation is that we shouldn't raise boys to become men overcome with animalistic rage. As Simone de Beauvoir might have it, one isn't born a beast but rather becomes one. Perhaps this isn't quite right. Maybe the most dangerous animal isn't a man with doors under his feet and walls in his fists, but a man on his knees, afraid of the ceiling, all too intimate with the earth.

/////

It is our luck as NDNs that the horizon of love is unreachable by ship or feet. When my ancestors had nothing, the night was still devoted to them, to being the body's negative space. We are children of war for whom the earth is a collaborative work of art. We fold the sky into little flowers and keep none to ourselves.

On the other hand, were I to write a Modern History of Gay Sex, I'd need to write of the kingless in a sprawling kingdom of shame and ecstasy. I'd need to write of the ecstasy of shame and the shame of ecstasy. Much of being a gay man in rural Canada is still the experience of being a stampede of horses in an enclosed cul-de-sac. The horses are invisible and translucent, but the pain of galloping through walls and furniture and fences is acute.

At Oxford, in my dorm at the city's western edge, I hungered for a language in which each syllable held at least another, so I habitually logged onto Grindr after midnight. A man said he wanted me to "manhandle" him (an idiom from the maw of a masculinist vernacular fine-tuned by gay men for decades). By manhandle, he could've meant a whirlwind of things: a brutal intimacy, plain ol' brutality, objectification, sadism, poetry, and so on. In my bed, ass up, face buried into a pillow, he was a monument to shame and, because of this, godly.

Giovanni's Room is a treatise on gay shame—an arousing, devastating, and frustrating novel about a closeted gay man who brandishes confusion like a bludgeon. With men, I don't feel shame; I rarely have. And so I don't intend to write a book about it. If anything, I'll write an ode to gay fugitivity. What freedom to be a horse!

FUTUROMANIA

As soon as someone dies, frenzied construction of the future (shifting furniture, etc.):
futuromania
—Roland Barthes, *Mourning Diary*

The aesthetic function of the novel, to my mind at least, is to
whisper, to hide critique, to grab a reader by the throat with
an invisible hand. I want no part in this. My provocations will
be bare-faced. I won't trick anyone. Maybe what I want is to
be violent in an *epistemic* sense; the blood will be not on my
hands but on my words. This is why I'm a poet before all else.
Maybe it's best if I admit everything that is fucked up about
me and my writing practice in the first paragraph of any piece
of writing. Am I fucked up because I believe beauty is in short
supply? That this lack is all I care to write about as of late?
That the world is at once the condition of possibility for and
addicted to this beautylessness? Probably. To be without beauty
is an integral component of human life in Canada. There, I said
it. Now no one needs to feel slowed down by this heretofore
unutterable sentence. This act of avowal is no heroic feat; my
desperation is creaturely. I spew verbal matter even when my
mouth is shut. Truth is I feel savaged by language, by the History
of Language, which is always-already a History of the NDN as
an Endangered Animal.

I'm a body of knowledge, not one of chemical compounds. Which is to say it is the fate of NDNs to live as ideas do. It is on the rez that one can hear words speak as though in a chorus. To tear the page is to tear our world apart. What shame to be a sentence on its knees! The day I obtained my driver's license, I followed a cumulus cloud through a maze of dirt roads until it evaporated. Forty minutes. That was all it took. I bore witness. No one asked this of me, but I wanted to keep watch of the dying everywhere, so I could figure out how to care for a bleeding sentence.

I admit to a friend that most days I feel like I'm sinking in on myself. She asks me to elaborate. I say, *I had a dream recently in which I was bent backward, my arms perpendicular to the floor. This is how I wander about,* I tell her. *What others see is out of sync with the interior of my body, which is rarely still or upright. It sounds to me,* she says, *like you're plagued by a kind of dysphoria with the world. Loneliness,* I wonder out loud. *Yes,* she answers, *yes. I'm reminded,* she adds, *of a line in Claudia Rankine's* Don't Let Me Be Lonely: *"deep within her was an everlasting shrug." Not a shrug,* I protest, *but a bark, a primal shout.* A beast of burden is a beast nonetheless.

I pull over to the side of a dirt road to change a flat tire. I'm in the middle of nowhere, which for some is all we have left and all there ever was. The tire isn't a tire but a balloon that cost one dollar and ninety-nine cents at a grocery store on the main street of nowhere. The balloon isn't filled with air but with grief. The grief isn't a response to just one event but to a continuance of events, a horrible rhythm of events. The tire that isn't a tire but a balloon pops and suddenly the heaviness of being is what tethers us to the earth while the world floats away. In the acoustic aftermath of the pop, in the cacophony of its wake, there is "pure gesture," there is a feral form of freedom.[1]

A structuralist on my worst days, I fixate on suffering's form, its toothy outline. This gets me nowhere but nowhere. The jury is still out on the question of whether function outweighs structure in the history of settler colonialism. Some say the fact of our killability and the fact of their bloodthirstiness is the ur-function. Others are inclined to flesh out the methods and ways of thinking of this prolonged manhunt, how it evolves and manifests where we can barely diagnose it. Regardless, that so few have packed their bags and left in opposition to this unethics of settlement is an affront to poetry. Is all Canadian poetry an incantatory performance of an impossible subject position? Not mine to answer once and for all, but I do read with a tilted head and squinted eyes. No matter how much of the literature of forgiveness I take in, which sings in a prayerful register, I can't shed this ancestral anger. I visited St. John's, Newfoundland, in the summer of 2018. An elected councilor mentioned that there had been an uproar in response to the city's routinized declaration that they sit atop the traditional lands of the Beothuk, now extinct. Fevered locals have called for archaeological evidence to prove this act of emplacement. The "now extinct," so carelessly narrated, so emptied of its terror, has been mostly wiped from the city's political imagination. They continue to build their lives in a bout of historical amnesia. The ungrievable, those of us who worship an impossible future, we who never were, are rarely granted as sizeable a public rage as theirs on that tiny, haunted island. This is our racialized burden, our embargoed emotivity. Your staying put isn't an innocent stance. Nothing will make this hurt less.

At the time of writing, no one is in an argument with Canada. Yet Canada has its gloved hands over its ears, as though someone were about to question why it is splayed out on a toilet like a widower on an open casket. Canada has yet to recoil at its reflection in the rear-view mirror. America, its deranged brother, is already engorged on itself like a nesting doll. Canada lives in my refrigerator. It spoils my groceries, just days old. It hangs, like a uvula, in my throat, governing my speech, draining it of its venom. Canada is more akin to noise pollution than the canopy of a boreal forest. Not a country, but a radioactive wolf in wolf's clothing.

I have a phobia of the police. How could I trust he who disavowed personhood to instead be a gun? He who is bullets rather than an organism capable of nurturance? To be a gun is to be against life. I want to be for life and to be against that which is against life. Living in a world where people are guns is a brutal legacy. To some, there is an incomprehensibility to this. Why divest oneself of the ethics of being a person and thus refuse to be open to the charity of those around you? A bullet is beholden to nothing, not even the barrel that births it. We can't ask a gun for forgiveness, as its maker has already been empowered by law to shed blame, to be blameless. (The police are outside the law because they administer it, regulate and deregulate its limits.) The police are, then, differently personed; they are without souls, thus incredibly ugly. I was about to say that this made them non-beings, but no, that is our imprint. This makes them beings writ large in a colonialist sense, the apogee of an ontology of modernity. The police are at the same time deader than even those of us who are the socially dead, interminably killable because of the codes of race and gender. The police don't live in the world or in a reality shared by others. The police are faceless, which engenders a Levinasian dilemma. With what do we signal our humanity in the line of fire of their guns? Forever isn't an impossibility for them. In a haven of infinitude, which isn't the world-as-it-is, the police are zombified. Zombies are at once beyond justice and its deranged progeny. Police are grievable subjects par excellence. Once the state manufactured a monopoly on grief, the marginalized went on embarrassing the privileged with our buckling, bullet-holed knees.

Roland Barthes's *Mourning Diary* is a record of a struggle with aliveness, a struggle that eschews and indeed consumes the primacy of writing. I, in my twenties, feel a lot like Barthes in his sixties, grief-stricken, without the nucleus of his affective life, his mother. In pursuit not of understanding but of misunderstanding, of a "sense of life," which is not "a life" because "a life" is too unmusical. Misunderstanding here doesn't mean confusion but rather a way of thinking that enables one to become one's "own mother" against the evidence that this is an unbearable project. There is, however, a key distinction: to be NDN is to be without a "sense of life" from the get-go. All of us are unlucky in that we make soggy memories in a weaponized loneliness that is irreversible. There is a "discontinuous character" not just to our mourning but also to our aging. In our homes, the furniture is always shifting while we sleep. I wake up and there's a sofa on top of me. The sofa is both a thought experiment of sorts and an emblem of the experience of NDN life, our tortured embodiment, our bodylessness, which is televised and made into bad art. We are without a flesh to signal our futurity, overwrought by signification, in the no man's land of a wild imaginary. Soon, there will be a sofa everywhere my shame grows: everywhere.

A conversation with a white male poet about Sheila Heti's *Motherhood* comes back to me. I mention that I think the novel is riveting in its restlessness and that Heti takes an ostensibly refined and knowable concept—motherhood—and disaggregates it, making it curiouser and thus open for resignification. *There's a cinematic quality to the experience of reading*, I tell him, *as though witnessing a sculptor at work. Right*, he says, *but I'm not sure I'll read on. To me, it boils down to the fact that there are just more important things to write about.* This signified to me that he'd been mothered by someone who seldom put pen to paper. This means that his mother didn't let him in on the open secret of her ugliness, which is what creative writing *does*—it traffics in ugly. In protest, I ask, *What about those for whom their mothers were passing cars or an open flame in the part of the brain where memories are made?* I wait for my skin to stretch itself over his, so that he can feel the panic I do, an accumulation of all the motherless men with whom I've spoken about matters of love and heartbreak. I take in emotional resonances of this sort, catalog them—this is my bioethics. I thought this was also my pedagogy of empathy. But there I was, flat on the floor—a question mark with fur.

Brennan Ahenakew, twenty, was found dead in a burnt-out car on the Ahtahkakoop Cree Nation. Three months later, the Royal Canadian Mounted Police (RCMP) ruled that "nothing indicate[d] foul play." You should know this by now: poetry is the act of "hearing beyond what we are able to hear."[2] With settler gossip of this nature, the RCMP sought to order grief, to pressurize the narrative and what could be publicly felt about Ahenakew and his loved ones. "Foul play" here is a well-oiled machine, hidden away from the discursive grid in which NDNs are made to live and die in ways that are without shock value. I dream in English and it is foul play. If I could free sense-making from the spell of the juridical and thus come to mediate what "foul" can incite, I would drag that burnt-out car across the prairies, through towns of no significance. With what remains, I would make another kind of music, one that would floor those within earshot, using only the ground beneath my feet. An ethnographic event. A revolutionary moment of acoustic violence. My music would be pungent and foggy. In the sensory world of my grief, there would be touch and sound and nothing else. My song would go on forever—"a future / music still unheard."[3] People would fall in love to it, sleep to it, have breakfast to it. Still, they would be corrupted by the hackneyed fact of their living. Too entangled in the world to write, caught up in a performance of unending sorrow, I would finally be a poet.

When I wake up, I think there should be flowers at my feet, but there never are. I could be a [insert overdetermined noun], and no one would be able to discern it, a starved nothingness spewing from my ears to no alarm. In my bedroom, the words "political" and "depressed" go hand in hand, as though to enunciate one is to mouth the other. This is the hallmark of institutional discourse. How much devastation can a word unleash? How much subtext can I hide under my armpits in a laboratory for excited speech? Sometimes I live not in an apartment but in a glass cube, as though exhibited in a museum of political depression. I lob words at the glass, though this is an inadequate characterization because what I do is both before and more than linguistic, a post-verbal conduct. I experiment with the intensity with which words launch out of me. A mouth is no longer a mouth when it twists language into something without and against form. A mouth is no longer a mouth when it can't hold back what is inside it.

Something happened in those death-schools that made happiness into a rotted thing. I smile now and it is still a rotten smile. My teeth are historical solidities. My breath reeks of the loneliness of living under a bed. I confused a man for a prairie sky. Up there, in him, how I hoped to have my soured breath drained out of me! At sunset, NDN boys look red, drenched in biopower. Our fury is animalistic. Can a poem resemble animality? Can a poem be resonant with it? Fury is a revolutionary habit. I have faith in the emancipatory power of rage and little else. In my fury, I'm differently gendered. I want to be a bad girl. I want to be a bad girl so there's a musicality to my rebellion. To be a bad girl is to be one of the most furious things in the modern world. To be a bad girl is to be one of the most admonished things in the modern world. A bad girl is she who has rid herself of the brutalities of socialization. No one will look at me adoringly and because of this I will be freed from the sovereign's clenched fist. The antithesis of the bad girl is the man who self-destructs. She savages the codes of gender; he is made rancid by them. It's too soon to tell what they together make possible in their wake. To be a bad girl is to be alive against the odds, a screeching question. Let me be a bad girl.

NDN writer bemoans the Red Condition, which is that wherever he goes he posits his queerness as a metaphysical conundrum. With each lispy word Modern History aggregates inside him like a wasp colony. Everywhere he is met by rows and rows of Michel Foucaults who promise he is freer than he thinks. NDN writer chuckles to himself now and then about the idiosyncrasy of this. NDN writer is reminded of Judith Butler who in *Gender Trouble* ruminates on what she calls the "sentimental" Foucault, the Foucault who despite his paranoid habits of diagnosis and disavowal sometimes paused and stood beside himself to nod to a less disciplinary elsewhere. Legendarily, Foucault seldom spoke about himself. He and NDN writer don't have this in common. But NDN writer does suspect that Foucault's sentimentality had everything to do with something he has already written down in another poem: no one runs to theory unless there is a dirt road in him. NDN writer is hard at work on the paradox that one can be born into a past and at the same time indecipherable to it. (That is his job: to keep watch of paradox.) NDN writer knows that this isn't a new undertaking. To be unoriginal might have humiliated NDN writer a few years ago, but it doesn't matter because today he's in a boat with a bunch of Foucaults minutes away from an island where the only universal is that there are no bodies to bury and thus no longer a need to make shovels out of our heavy hands.

White empathy razes everything in its path. Since I can remember, the world hasn't lasted longer than a single day before it was flushed down the toilet. I take in the news south of the border. I take in the news of the border, the ongoingness of its terror. Knives flower from the soles of my feet. Even my tiptoeing is a kind of violence. I don't shed a tear about this. I cry about other matters: that so much of being alive in the Americas is about playing dead. To go about the drudgery of the day, I have to at least marginally play dead to white anger and white sovereignty and white hunger and white forgiveness and white innocence. If one is alive to all these rabid emotions all the time, one experiences the world as though it were nothing but TV static. It's a sedative, so indifference is no armor. That my heart beats loudly doesn't immunize me from the static or lessen its grip on my well-being. I understand this to be my Canadian inheritance.

Until today, I railed against the grisly fate reserved for men like me. I'm an anachronism in the way that all queer men are anachronisms—far too early. I'm a poet in the way that all queer men are poets (not a novel thought, likely). Ours is the audacity of begging for "a compassionate / wilderness."[4] José Esteban Muñoz: "The queer citizen-subject labors to live in a present that is calibrated . . . to sacrifice our liveness."[5] I don't need a record of my here-ness. What I do need is to take ecstasy with José Esteban Muñoz. Paradise is wherever he is. Until then, I will try to be a pretty wound at least once.[6] Confession: I'm not yet comfortable taking my shirt off in a poem. Subjectivity abuses. Subjectivity rescues. Men shoved my head into the clouds. I missed so much. There is humiliation in this dystopia, too. Here, my words appear in the air, upside down:

My mouth is a dirty floor. I'm sweeping up the dirt with my imagination.

GAY: 8 SCENES

1.

I'm a closeted teen. From the non-place where psychic life and carnality meet, I muster the might to look into the mirror and mime an unutterable sentence: *I am gay.* The words crowd my mouth but can only thicken into sound from somewhere else, as if ventriloquized. Language and gesture are too open to appropriation, too prone to misuse, so I have nowhere or nothing with which to do the deeply human work of self-making. My first territory of desire is the territory of me. Ocean Vuong: "A safe moment is a moment where we are in control of our pleasure, of our own joy." Vuong calls masturbation "a place where we are safest to ourselves."[1] In his "Ode to Masturbation" he writes, "& sometimes / your hand / is all you have / to hold / yourself to this / world."[2] I gave a quirky and discomfiting talk at the 2016 gathering of the Native American and Indigenous Studies Association in Honolulu called "Anarchic Objects and the Autoerotics of Decolonial Love," in which I argued that indigeneity is an erotic concept. Against the sexual pulse of coloniality, its perverse sensuality and all that it elaborates in NDN social worlds, we have the safe haven of us, this flesh, however caught up in the sign systems of race we are. In this talk, I drew on Eve Kosofsky Sedgwick's *A Dialogue on Love*, in which she writes, "I was somebody who, given the opportunity, would spend hours and hours a day in my bedroom masturbating. Really. Hours and hours." She continues by way of a haiku: "It's something that I could / yearn toward and be / lost in the atmosphere of / To me, a whole world."[3] These theories of masturbation nod to the geographies of joy that manifest where we are trained not to see them. Remember: we need to keep watch of our own pleasures.

2.

It's April 2014. I finish my third year of undergraduate studies at the University of Alberta. I expand with sexual possibility. Which is another way of saying I'm incredibly horny. I have little sexual experience, but I'm not technically a virgin. I have not slept with anyone in Edmonton; I'm an Edmonton virgin. I download Grindr. For my profile picture I use a tightly framed shot of my torso with the waistband of a jockstrap peeking out at the bottom of the screen. Almost immediately my phone buzzes with a message from a similarly beheaded torso: *hey, looking?* He has a couple of abs, which already makes me feel as though I'm touring through a foreign world. He doesn't have a car and can't host me at his apartment, so he suggests we fuck in the exercise room in the basement of his building, which he presses is rarely used, especially so late on a weeknight. This jettisons me outside the neighborhood of old feeling, where there is nothing but red flags, somewhere outside ordinary time. I vibrate with worry so much that it feels like my skin is loosening. I pick him up and drive back to my apartment, where I unfold into him, without grace, like a crumpled map, long discarded. He keeps asking what gets me hard, but I have almost no experiential knowledge to mine to hear the question. This will be the start of a hard-worn habit of setting myself on fire in dimly lit bedrooms all over Edmonton. I become that fire before I have the emotional intelligence to perceive it as such. So many world-shattering things can happen in the schism between an event and our ability to comprehend it. I pitch a tent there. It is years before I relocate, before I'm evicted.

3.

D is the first man I fall in love with. I write about him all the time, even when I'm not writing about him. Like all my would-be boyfriends in the period between 2014 and 2016, I meet him on Grindr. His messages are short but wayward, direct but quietly bizarre. We grab coffee at a shop near my apartment. I'm fixed by quirky facets of his appearance, which don't align with his muted personality: a tattoo on the top of his ear that reads GANGSTA; his barren blue eyes, which ward off attention more than they invite it; his Lululemon top and pants in conflicting shades of blue. *You're gorgeous*, he says, to evolve the awkward back-and-forth into something riskier. We laze about on the lawn in the front of a university, which is when he decides he wants to date me. I don't say anything, but we kiss nonetheless. A few days later he tells me he loves me, a confession that throws me, for we have yet to sink into the mutual debt that comes from months of care-giving and re-subjectification. At a restaurant, I ask him to invite me into the world of him, to open himself up to observation. He begins by telling me about the storied tattoos peppering his body—I remember none but the name MICHAEL etched across the small of his back, which commemorates an ex-boyfriend and a relationship that sounds eerily like ours. This unleashes a flurry of entangled vignettes about his life, including a summer-long stint in the British porn industry. (I refuse to view the footage when offered; there's something about the way porn shores up the performativity of intimacy that makes my heart sink. How was I to know the difference between porn-D and boyfriend-D?) He then moves on with trepidation to the loss of both his mom and younger sister to suicide. With self-deprecating humor, he confesses that this is why he's so fucked up. He has known nothing but unbearable grief all his adult life, which pulls him into the emotional house of men like me. Terese Marie Mailhot: "I realized that love can be mediocre and a safe comfort, or it can be unhinged and hurtful. Either seemed like a good life."[4] Except for D, there would be no good life, just a depleted world. I ask, *How do you know you love me?* He doesn't answer. Later he gives me a cheap-and-dirty response from the bargain bin of capitalist feeling—*I love you because you do so much for me.*

We never fuck because his anti-depressants suppress his libido, but we spend a lot of time together naked, loitering in the bombed-out visual field of us. "That our eyes stopped / believing in what was in front of us / was the closest we got to killing ourselves."[5]

Fast-forward to the fall of 2017. I'm driving home from the university. I turn a corner that will put me on a straight path to my apartment building. Suddenly, shatteringly, I lock eyes with him, standing at an intersection. Until then, I had a suspicion he was either institutionalized or dead. He is neither, just impossibly alive. He doesn't recognize me.

4.

At first queerness was guesswork, a series of mistakes that led
me to dating a swath of white men who teetered between two
poles: fetishization and color-blindness. One white man from
Atlantic Canada spoke proudly about how all his male partners
had been NDN, unable to diagnose his own desires as dehu-
manizing, unable to discern that when he fucked me he made
me into a moaning object. Another didn't believe that racial difference affected the texture of intimate life, insisting he pre-
ferred not to think of me as Cree, as someone whose capacity
for love was bound up in his differential exposure to violence.
In their minds, we were inside an experiment, one in which they
could sculpt better, more cultured selves. I, however, was inside
a proxy war, fending off yet another assault on NDN livability.
Neither understood themselves to be my enemies. Soon after
breaking up with the latter, I slept with another NDN for the
first time. We met on OkCupid. We spent about a week tex-
ting, ruminating on the difficulties of interracial care, how it
demanded us to be larger than we were and shrank us all at once.
Together we created a form of vulnerability that we wanted to
nest inside, not one that injured us. It was the small things in our
brief time spent with each other that illuminated the possibilities
of decolonial love—the talk of how the reserve is a lighthouse
that beckons us now and then; the jokes about what it's like to
be visibly NDN on dating apps, which are programmed at the
levels of visuality and data collection to invite racism. Despite
having to lie in a bed with history,[6] we—two NDN boys who
needed to be saved just as much as we needed to do the saving—
fucked in the name of queer NDN joy. On my knees, before
him, he taught me how to long as though longing alone could
propel me into the future. Until then, intimacy had been a lost
country. I was becoming vivid to the world. Oh, how I wanted
to remember everything before it happened. Oh, how tightly
I shut my eyes.

5.

Lisa Duggan: "We have been administered a kind of political sedative—we get marriage and the military then we go home and cook dinner, forever."[7] At the core of homonormativity is an erotics of whiteness, which designates some bodies as undesirable, too submerged in the dirty waters of signification to rescue. This was one of the hardest lessons to learn, that a persecuted people could reinscribe the violence of ontological shaming. Judith Butler probes the limits of "outness": "Who is represented by *which* use of the term [queer], and who is excluded? For whom does the term present an impossible conflict between racial, ethnic, or religious affiliation and sexual politics? What kinds of policies are enabled by what kinds of usages, and which are backgrounded or erased from view?"[8] Queers who ride the advantageous waves of whiteness slide smoothly into the depths of the normative. This is done at the expense of racial flourishing. On dating apps, where white men hide behind a veil of anonymity but discriminate out in the open, this identity crisis wages on—"NO FATS, NO FEMS, NO ASIANS" is a banner under which white men build a dystopia. I could recite the vulgar speech that's been hurled at me, but I won't. There's too much to mine in them from those who feed, like vampires, on the spoils of injurious information. Of course this doesn't negate the violence entirely—it lingers as a specter, tied to the bank of memories we have about vicious language. Perhaps that specter is politically volatile enough to arouse a sense of injustice to end the slow making of a queer future replete with racism. Maggie Nelson: "And what kind of madness is it anyway, to be in love with something constitutionally incapable of loving you back?"[9] Has anyone ever managed not to mold the body into an archive of their own degradation?

6.

It's January 2017 and I'm living in Oxford, England. I have a fuck buddy who's from Estonia, where his family of animists, witches, and shamans have lived for centuries. He bikes to my dorm, stinking with loneliness. Among a flurry of words, we, a soon-to-be-anthropologist and a student of feminist theory, talk about Cree language families and the heavy atmosphere of daily life in Oxford, how it thickens with racial matter. As fuck buddies do, we dance to a YouTube mix of techno songs from 2016. This blurs into something else. You get the gist. We—two men, both at least one hundred and seventy pounds, both at least six feet tall—sleep on my twin-sized bed, as though the next day were a Sunday and there were only Sundays from here on out.

7.

In the west end of Edmonton, my boyfriend and I are holding hands as I drive to the movie theatre on a sweltering August afternoon. We are stopped at a red light when a white heterosexual couple in a rusted pickup truck scan us as one might an abstract painting in a gallery: puzzled, repulsed by the unknowability of what's before them. Instinctually I peer over and catch their frenzied glares. I turn into a wounded animal feral with insecurity. *What empowers them to look at us with the fury of history?* I say out loud, to no one, not even my boyfriend, who's erring on the side of optimism. I've been made into a toppled statue too many times to join him there. They lag as the light turns green, which allows them to pull behind me. Changing lanes when I do, turning when I do, they communicate to me without words that nothing, even if installed with the sentimentality of poetry, will dial back this sort of road rage. I imagine myself yelling lines of poetry as a last-ditch attempt to signal to them my and his and our humanity. Eventually a yellow light separates us, and my boyfriend and I exhale again. That night I sleep not with him but with the thought of what they could have done to us, what they wanted to do to us. From nowhere but the graveyard of history could someone marshal the cruelty of denying someone the solidity of everyday life. The biopower of each and every "faggot" hurled at me at the grocery store, at the university, in northern Alberta, courses through my veins, making my body feel too much like a body, a feeling I've wanted to evade my entire life.

8.

I'm a love-drunk thing, so I'm to be but found wanting. To be found wanting is to be caught red-handed. To be red-handed and to want not in the register of the here and now but in the then and there is an NDN fate to which I'm obedient.

How to account for the love that bubbles up where it is banned? We visit in the back alleys of the world, where those who have been caged in the visual register of nothingness gather, against the de-democratization of the ability to world, in a common worldlessness, armed only with our wordiness.

NDN Utopia is a world away, Love announces. *Skoden,* Heartbreak responds, pointing his lips upward, knowing fully that it isn't that simple, but also that it is indeed that simple.

LONELINESS IN THE AGE OF GRINDR

It's 2014. I hook up with men I don't find attractive because I suspect they've been told they aren't thin enough, toned enough, tall enough, pretty enough, or white enough to fuck. I take on a liberal savior complex. I commit to the idea that my body can be the conduit through which they learn to love their own. I think I owe them my flesh because they find me desirable when what I see is a knot of contradictions and sour myths. I quickly become an expert in the discipline of sacrifice. What's the word for when you fuck not out of arousal but a hunger for hunger? Don't call it desperation; too many wish to romanticize an NDN boy's experience of self-destruction.

I allow myself to tiptoe into economies of desire in which I'm a fetish or a compromise, which is to say I always melt into the mattress. Sometimes I'm told I'm beautiful or sexy, and for a long time this compels me to kiss the bloody lips of precarity day in and day out. This is the precarity of treating the body as though it were a catch-22. What is chronic loneliness if not the desire to exist less and less, to deplete little by little? Maggie Nelson: "I have been trying, for some time now, to find dignity in my loneliness. I have been finding this hard to do."[1]

////

In the aftermath of the AIDS epidemic, Grindr users fuck in the specter of sexual infection. DDF—drug- and disease-free—is a high-velocity acronym that not only presupposes that sexually active users are regularly tested but also that these tests occur outside the time frame during which a blood test likely won't yield a proper diagnosis. For gay and queer men and their sex partners, it's as though Grindr users were paradoxically infected and not at the same time. Public health stokes the flames of this discourse too. I've never donated blood, for example, given the restrictions placed on those like me in Canada who have the kind of sex I do. When paired with the sexual purchase of men who are white, muscular, neuro-typical, and straight-acting, Grindr morphs into something of a geography of anxiety. Our bodies—possibly contagious, possibly spoiled by the sign system of race—are disavowed, again and again. Grindr's archival form—its very condition of possibility—generates encounters that might be racially and/or sexually polluting. This brings about strangulated forms of sociality: (1) of worrying, even if your sex acts were harm reductive, that your body could be destroying you from the inside; and (2) of wanting bodies made desirable as an effect of the sexual histories of colonialism and white supremacy. In this configuration, sex is always a guessing game ruled by risk. With risk as one of the primary engines of sexual life, a body isn't a body but a battlefield.

////

It's deep into August 2015. I'm about to leave my apartment to welcome incoming First Nations, Métis, and Inuit students to the University of Alberta. Out of habit, I check Grindr. Almost immediately, I receive a message from an attractive white guy who had written to me a couple weeks back. The right mix of lonely, horny, and heartbroken justifies the possibility of a last-minute hookup. I was already going to be a few minutes late anyway.

You looking? he asks.

Yeah, you, I respond, even though I should be out the door.

Yeah. I'm so fucking horny. You a bottom? Home alone?

Yeah, I bottom. Want to come over? I answer, maybe too quickly. *What's your address?*

Grindr users don't mince words. The app has made sex easy to come by for men who've been told their desires were to be shunned from public life. Sex, or something akin to it, will make you abandon in an instant the "you" you've sculpted over years.

I send the stranger my address, and he shows up about fifteen minutes later. (My instinct is to suggest that anonymous sex pressurizes the figure of the stranger, makes it into a pleasurable category.) I feel as though I'm selling a false product, that I'm not his type, that he can fuck someone better looking. So when he does show up, I've already decided I will bend backward for him, literally and figuratively. It's only 10 a.m., but he looks as though he hasn't yet slept. He's sweaty and fidgety, as though racked by street drugs. I know this isn't the ideal situation to put myself in, but I can't pass him up. Ideality, I reason, is an arbitrary qualifier anyway.

He's about five-ten, thin with a six-pack and light brown hair. His eyes are large and blue, and he's wearing sweatpants and a hoodie, both of which somehow make his slender body look sculptural. He's a twink, one of the most fuckable body types in the Grindr universe.

I didn't think you'd come, I admit, self-deprecatingly.

Oh, why's that? he fires back, winking at me.

Because you hadn't said you were actually on your way, I lie. We laugh. I want to cry.

Here we are, I say as we enter my two-bedroom apartment. I let myself into my head to note that this feels like a cheap, amateur porno.

I immediately take him into my spare bedroom and unzip my jean shorts. You learn to cut to the chase in the drama of hookup culture. I'm wearing a jockstrap, which he requested, but nonetheless I feel like an erotic being in one, a rare occurrence. He makes me into a one-sided object of his desire by ceasing to say more than a couple words at a time to me. He turns me around to push me onto the bed. He alternates between licking my asshole and pushing his finger in. He then jumps onto the bed to shove his large dick into my mouth—pictures of which admittedly caught my attention during our earlier chats. He thrusts his dick into my throat despite the gag reflex it elicits. He coaxes a pulsating vulnerability out of me and this turns him on. I can feel tears welling up in my eyes, but I don't want him to stop. I want to feel as though he can snap me in half. He bends me over again and rubs his dick on my butt. I don't feel comfortable anymore, but I don't let him know this either. He jerks off, and, without warning, ejaculates on my asshole. I don't notice until he puts his clothes on.

That was weird, he says, breaking the silence.

What do you mean?

I mean it wasn't weird, but I usually don't cum that quickly.

Did you cum on my ass? I ask, knowing the answer.

Yeah, sorry about that, that usually doesn't happen. He laughs. *I didn't even get to fuck you*, he adds, registering to me that he doesn't comprehend the depth of my question.

I feel violated. I grab the Kleenex box next to the bed to wipe my ass, cautiously, methodically, so as to avoid semen sliding inside my anus. I head to the bathroom to use the adult cleansing wipes I'd recently bought. When I go back into the living room, he asks if I have water. Sweating and out of breath, he drinks the bottle's contents in one gulp. I still have to make it to the university, so I walk with him to the elevator.

Once there, I make poor use of my words and ask him if he's clean.

Yeah. Well, I mean I hope so, he jokes. I spill onto the floor.

I wouldn't have let you do that if you had asked. Cum on my ass, I mean, I respond, frustrated, sick with worry.

Oh, well I guess that makes sense, he says, without compassion.

Standing in the lobby, we say goodbye to each other. I never see him again.

////

Hospitals have always been enemy territory. My body, too brown to be innocent, enflames the nurses' racialized curiosities. For them, there's always the possibility that my pain is illusory, dreamt up in order to get my next fix. Or maybe I just want somewhere warm to sleep because the world is too hard on an NDN like me. This is never the case, for me at least, but their imaginations run wild nonetheless.

I jump into my car and begin frantically searching Google to gauge the "severity" or "riskiness" of the hookup. Most websites I visit suggest readers seek medical attention to see if they're eligible for PEP, or post-exposure prophylaxis, an antiretroviral drug that can prevent HIV from latching onto your body if administered quickly enough, usually within forty-eight hours of exposure. Instead of going to the university, I email a colleague to cancel five minutes before I'm due to speak. I drive to the STI Clinic, which is hidden at the back of an old and low-functioning downtown hospital. Filled with bodies confronted by their sexual histories, the STI Clinic is not my favorite place to visit. You have to go through a loading dock to get to it; once inside, you walk past the patrons, who avoid making eye contact. The receptionist, located behind a Plexiglas window (which seems antithetical to a more ethical, more feminist hospital), asks what your reason for visiting is, as if it could be anything. I tell the receptionist I have questions about PEP and that I'm hoping to see a nurse. She looks puzzled but pages a nurse anyway.

With a nurse, I replay the event: his semen, I sheepishly confess, likely got inside my anus. She asks if I'd been penetrated, to which I say *technically, no*. She points out that if my anus hadn't been penetrated, it was unlikely semen had entered my bloodstream. She explains that PEP is only administered to patients whose risk of infection is exceptional: a prisoner raped by an HIV-positive inmate, for example. The drug, too expensive to be handed out to anyone with anxiety, needs to be approved by Alberta Health Services. Nonetheless, she suggests that I visit an emergency department to get a second opinion from a doctor.

They might approve you. I would give it a shot, she concedes.

I wait an hour in the emergency room at the University of Alberta Hospital. I ask the nurse at the triage station when I might see a doctor. She tells me that I likely won't see one for at least three hours, that my case is not life-or-death, that I'm still breathing, and that the doctor would likely send me away untreated. She suggests I make use of the STI Clinic downtown. I might not die in the lobby, I think to myself, but a world is still in the balance. I leave despite myself.

I work on campus for an hour, then drive to a nearby walk-in clinic. I can't shake the pestering sense that something is amiss. The receptionist asks for a reason for my visit.

I'd like to ask a couple questions about my sexual health, I say, trying to maintain at least a sliver of secrecy in the small room peopled to capacity.

Oh, like STDs? she wonders aloud, without concern for my privacy.

Yup. I clear my throat.

I explain what has unfolded to a doctor whose attention seems to be elsewhere. I ask if she knows about PEP and she admits that she doesn't, that she's just returned from the Middle East and that cases like mine didn't come up there. Men in the Middle East are having gay sex, I think to myself, but she probably wasn't a doctor they felt comfortable seeking help from.

It feels as though I'm utterly without agency in the face of an ignorant doctor who has little knowledge about harm reduction. After I note the worry that I can't shoulder alone, she excuses herself to contact Alberta Health Services. The walls, paper thin, can't conceal the irritation in her voice. Speaking to a nurse, she says she doesn't want to waste anyone's time with such a silly matter. Her footsteps approach.

You'll have to wait about eight to ten weeks to be tested, she says, coldly.

Thanks, I manage, half-heartedly.

I don't think about sex for weeks without a wave of anxiety overpowering my libido. Han Kang: "*I hold nothing dear. Not the place where I live, not the door I pass through every day, not even, damn it, my life.*"[2]

////

My story, I now understand from a distance, was one of the unequal distribution of public knowledge around sexual health. I was being conscripted into a culture of fear that makes STIs such as HIV into public enemies. Without care, there is no room for harm reduction. What's more, I had no audience for my misery. With no one around to apprehend the exigencies of my emotional tumult, everywhere I went became a zone of abandonment. How was I who was barely enclosed in an "I" supposed to trudge through solitude's thick overgrowth?

////

Since, I've been fixated on the loneliness of being denied care where it is said or expected to be integral to a social operation. From the deleterious way men vie for sex to the room for disregard in the medical world, care is withheld or obliterated in an existential way, stripping some of sovereignty to the extent that we put a ban on the production of joy. Jill Stauffer gets at something like this with her concept of "ethical loneliness," which for her is "the isolation one feels when one, as a violated person or as one member of a persecuted group, has been abandoned by humanity, or by those who have power over one's life's possibilities."[3] It's during moments when the self is negotiated with others—in sex, in medicine and public health—that one is prone to being pulled off course and thrown into a crisis of ontological proportions. I thus see it as my job to lay bare the catastrophic conditions that meet those who are wrenched into a world of loneliness where there are no bodies, just burning houses built from scratch.[4]

FRAGMENTS FROM A HALF-EXISTENCE

During a summer of sadness, I tried week after week to write a novel. The novel, which regularly changed form and genre and temporal structure and so on, was always about a previous relationship that happily unmoored me from a world I had lost interest in but nonetheless returned to out of a survival instinct that emboldened me to put trust in nostalgia.

I believed the quirk that made novelists novelists was an ability to say no to the world. But as a poet, I couldn't break the habit of trying to make the world and thus my lived life into an art object. I said yes to the world again and again, sometimes to my detriment, if only to increase the volume of my selfhood, a performance of creativity I felt closer to than invention. One night in an empty bed (empty beds are for me a call to art-making in response to an imposed quietude) it occurred to me that what I wanted wasn't to write a novel but to fall in love. Both were overwhelmingly possible, which perhaps explains why I accomplished neither.

A short example of one failed attempt:

> The end of one month bled into the other, my "I" bled into his, and before I knew it I was fucking a man in my parents' guest bedroom, his tiny body perched so gracefully on me that his thrumming arms looked like wings. All the daylight lacerated by the blinds dripped onto his slender face. He growled as he pushed down onto me, a song of ontological compromise. A body atop another is an elegiac gesture.

"So many things seem filled with the intent /
to be lost that their loss is no disaster."[1] He
maintains a hard-on by spitting into my mouth,
so I pretend there is a dried-up lake inside me.
I close my eyes and say, *I've been thinking about
you. I'm right here*, he answers. *I'm right here.
Open your eyes.*

My next attempt I believed at the time would rush out of me
onto the page because it bore a narrative structure that hypo-
thetically could reproduce itself without becoming monoto-
nous. The concept was that an art history student has sex with
a series of middle-aged white men who fetishize NDNs as
a commentary on the erotics of race, on sex as a performance
of race that is always uneven and a flattening of subjectivity for
the racialized:

Sweating, oranged by a bedside lamp, it looks
as though flames are tiptoeing onto him. He
tosses words at me, but the crackle of vaporiz-
ing wood drowns them out. I'm always hearing
more than what's hearable. It's an artist's duty
to refuse to be sedated by the real. If materiality isn't the arbiter of sense, then a gaseous
substance hissing at me in a stranger's home is
as routine as a bird's song at daybreak. My ears
heat up. I don't budge.

His apartment is in a state of disarray, an
accumulative kind, symptomatic of a life
staged in the throes of an indefatigable longing for that which hums with impossibility. The
roughly six-hundred-square-foot space can
hold neither more nor less than the grief of a
single, self-loathing white man. His bedroom
strains at its borders, barely able to suppress the

emotional innards. A damp bath towel hanging from the lip of a bathroom door is his poetry. A throat cleared before he greets me after an afternoon and evening of no conversation is his sad music. Towers of novels hazardously constructed everywhere are the bounds of his armyless kingdom.

A pang of vigilance, like a hand extended out from under me, tugs me back into his queen-sized bed, wide enough to be a monument to a lover who never arrived. Each fold in the fitted sheet has been won in a proxy war. The instigator, desire, hangs from the ceiling, grinning and bloodless. The weather here, I note, is sour. I shouldn't loiter lest I risk contamination. Unfreedom is contagious.

In my periphery, little pools of semen vibrate on his torso. He tracks my line of sight, which he interprets as interrogative, raising his right eyebrow in response. He tells me, defensively, that he was once toned but has since bloated with time.

He eyes me with a curiosity that I sense teeters between ferocity and emptiness depending on his sexual interest in the beheld. Tonight it's like a densely populated city, unpredictable and engulfing.

To disturb his gaze, I ask, from the edge of the mattress, "What's on your mind?"

He inhales like a singed tree. The textuality of his inhalation is a clue. He inches up the wall slowly until he is sitting upright. The semen dances. He rubs the back of his neck, smirks. A choreography of lust.

"First time I've slept with an NDN," he says, then winks.

Be the mouth of an ordinary river, my inner self instructs. Be not a gust of wind but the field of crops it brings to the ground in reverence and fear.

"What's the verdict?" The cadence of the sentence indicates amusement in spite of myself.

He hesitates. "You want the truth?"

I don't. "Absolutely."

"Well, I immediately got an erection when I read your ethnicity on Grindr, perhaps because I've been hooking up with dudes for decades now but none have been NDN. That made you interesting and strange and, and, uh, impossible. You were NDN, which meant that anything was possible because I had nothing against which to measure how sex with you might feel."

Were? He continues. "Then there you were, at my door, beautiful and, uh, fragile and attention-seeking, like an open window." That he is a man of letters doesn't ease me into his delicately spun discourse of race and eros. Sex can transform any and all into a starved, many-headed beast.

It dawns on me that I've been forced into the graveyard shift of a narrative of liberal empathy and personal development. I shove my legs into my jeans as he drones on. His voice wanes. He apologizes if he has offended me. I assure him he hasn't.

When I leave, I kiss him on the lips as though

they're a country to which I have pledged, as though I'll return. I won't.

I didn't ask for his name, so the pronouns he and him and his will have to do in this telling. Indeed, they've already done the job. And, like most things left unnamed, he will live on in my world as substance for creative labor and nothing else.

When I shut the door behind me I leave a cheap imitation of myself inside.

I have no one to ask if it's bad writing or not. I put it here because I suspect it doesn't matter.

////

Titles of novels I have tried to write thus far:
- *Critical Race Theory*
- *The Museum of Political Depression*
- *A Beast of Burden Is a Beast Nonetheless*
- *Bad Lover*
- *It's Lonely to Be Alive!*

////

The summer I had hours-long anal sex while battling a bout of hemorrhoids was an object lesson in entropy. The rectum is an affective sinkhole. *There is a big secret about sex: most people don't like it,*[2] I mumble to myself as blood drips from me into a toilet. I'm a sculpture on which the artist chose not to leave a signature. If I continue to romanticize sex, to pontificate in public about how it combats the suffocations of individuality, it's because sex is one of few social interactions I choose that reminds me of my unending penetrability. When I'm tangled in the body of another, something inside me shouts: *Even your precarious psyche isn't yours to mother!*

/////

Foucault is a Libra and this matters to me. I had been at times ambivalent and at others hostile to the astrological renaissance at the core of contemporary queer life. It seemed to me to be a kind of cop-out, in that it allows droves of internet users to think themselves outside the structures and political forces that constrict the world. The notion that one's disposition could be predetermined by the cosmos is orthodox and fatalist, two characteristics I never want attributed to me or my work. But then I came across a tweet that listed philosophers and their astrological signs. Foucault is a Libra and so am I. There is a kind of kinship in this that I don't want to lose. Had I been given the name Michel, this wouldn't have ensnared me to Foucault the way our dates of birth do. He is a theorist of freedom, and so am I. This is our lot as Libras.

An ex-boyfriend and I share the same date of birth, October 21. I took this coincidence to be a sign of our compatibility as lovers, which to some might constitute a lapse in judgment on my part. Wasn't I an empiricist who sneers at a notion as immaterial as happenstance? But the theorists who excite me most are, in a sense, speculative fiction writers. What's missing or fleeting in the world is evidence of other ways of being, of something dawning, so the onus isn't to observe a phenomenon as it happens but to chase after a hunch or a half-formed hypothesis that might accumulate into an artifact of a future history. Their keywords include possibility, utopia, futurity, hope, and optimism. This chorus of artist-thinkers taught me to be apprehensive about the tyranny of the material and to daydream about the underbelly of maps, about that which congregates just below the threshold of visibility. Perhaps this romance with the not-yet makes me a bad lover. So be it.

////

A man and I talked on the phone nightly, not because our lives were extravagant or torrid enough to warrant daily dispatches, but because we were planted in a narrative that was predictable, one in which we felt caressed. There was some end, however nebulous and inchoate, toward which we were heading. When the sex inevitably became procedural, I didn't soliloquize about the rise and fall of spontaneity. It wasn't a sign of doom, but a victory, a transcendence of promiscuity. Things happened I could anticipate. Finally, I was a part of a form in which I could suspend myself. In those days I was astute at the art of destroying myself without resorting to self-destruction. In the eyes of a man I didn't trust, I was a glistening tragedy.

////

My kink is the annihilation of my core sense of self. On Tinder, I swipe right on post-structuralists and no one else. I'm looking for someone with whom to rent an apartment at the intersection of fissured systems of meaning. Queer as in my attraction to you is an attraction to concepts for which you are a practical substitute.

////

My sadness is an elongated state of emergency. I dream in the color of sadness. I speak the bastardized language of sadness.

When I first moved to Edmonton, at just seventeen, I had a recurring dream. In it I watch, as though in front of a movie theatre screen, future-me (he looked identical to me then, but taller and wider, like a child's vision of aging) happen upon past-me, frail, skeletal, in a farmer's field, a small house in the periphery, canola sprouting around me and me, around them. Future-me's face is stoic, having perhaps resigned himself to the terror of what's to follow. From a bird's-eye view, I see future-me bend down slowly, pick up past-me, and then softly kiss his forehead. Future-me puts past-me back on the ground. He places his hands on past-me's papery chest, pushing him into the soil. (In the dream I can't scream or move.) Then, poof, they're both gone. But, just as quickly, I appear again, a blade of grass caught between the rusty teeth of morning.

////

Grad school was the wrong place for someone like me with an appetite for the utopian. But I was an idea in love with an idea—where else was I supposed to shelter this form of love?

////

iawîyak kanihtâ mihtâtahk = a body made of regret.

////

Cultural theorist Sianne Ngai defines "stuplimity" as an experience of boredom that is overwhelming, excessive, against calm. Sometimes I'm so bored with my puny life that it feels as though the roof above me is going to cave in. When not distracted by the noise of the social, life looms over me, like a single rain cloud.

Perhaps my next book will be about the fury that NDNs sublimate to go about being in a world we didn't want (a line of inquiry that repeats in almost all my writing). My book would be a speech act unto itself in that I would unleash that fury onto the page. It wouldn't, however, help people live better, and because of this it would be a failed text. Han Kang wrote a book called *The White Book* (translated from the Korean by Deborah Smith) that likely does help people live better. She's unflinching in her exploration of what it is to grow up inside a story of grief, of what it is to live in a place without boundedness where old memories materialize en masse. In a section called "Lace curtain" she meditates on what "a freshly laundered bed linen" can come to connote: "You are a noble person. Your sleep is clean, and the fact of your living is nothing to be ashamed of."[3] Although it's beautifully rendered, I would want to turn this observation inside out, for I'm prone to spoiling even well-nourished words. The governing thesis of my book would be that we aren't noble people and therefore the fact of our living is something to be ashamed of. The question I'd ask: What might it look like for NDNs to refuse life in the wake of all that's happened to us in a country in which we're social experiments before all else?

/////

A note on craft. In *Ban en Banlieue*, Bhanu Kapil writes, with wounding accuracy, "It's so quiet before a book begins. / So quiet that when my nervous system hurts, so does the sentence, because that's all we have: each other. The sentence and I. We cope."[4]

////

If I try to compose anything but sad poems, I fear it'll be akin to a widower trying to convince others that he has found happiness again by wearing a T-shirt that says HAPPINESS.

////

Why poetry? It allows for a romance of the negative that doesn't foreclose the possibility of a non-cruel kind of optimism.

The political climate in which art is made will determine whether poetry is a unit of accusation or revelation. I'm writing a literature of blame, for the record.

To my mind, one of the most vital modalities of decolonial life is that of remaining unaddressable to a settler public that feasts on our misery. Most of the time, writing a book seems incompatible with this.

////

At the book launch of *This Wound Is a World*, a white woman begged me not to kill myself. What this meant is that I hadn't yet died in a bewildering way. Then and now, I was and am a statistical and sociological feat. What she saw where my body should have been was an outline of a body crowded with indicators of my expiration date. She heard the terrible music not of a desire for another world but of a premature death, a mangling. I should have asked her to lament herself, her Canadian looking practice.

////

On a full midday flight from Toronto to Edmonton.
WHITE LADY: (*leans into me*) Is Edmonton home?
ME: (*restrained*) Yes.

WHITE LADY: Did you have a nice time in Toronto?

ME: (*pulls headphone out of right ear*) I was in Ottawa, actually. Just connecting.

WHITE LADY: Oh! What were you doing in Ottawa?

ME: I was at a literary festival—I'm a writer.

WHITE LADY: Do you have a book? What is it called?

ME: *This Wound Is a World.*

WHITE LADY: (*her eyes widen*) Oh!—*This Wound Is a World* . . . What's it about?

ME: It's, uh, I'm Indigenous—it has a lot to do with colonialism.

WHITE LADY: I teach therapists at the University of _____, and recently a number of elders helped me really rethink how trauma affects Indigenous peoples. Trauma isn't something you acquire—

[In my head, I think: "you" as in "me" specifically?]

WHITE LADY: —trauma is literally *who you are.*

(*An announcement by a flight attendant takes her attention elsewhere. Later, over Winnipeg, she asks if she can purchase food for me.*)

Encounters of this sort are like a leg stuck out in front of you. You self-interrogate, are made to suspend yourself in an existential limbo. There's the material you in the airplane who is called into an openness you have no power over, then the abstract you the white woman conjures from a bank of public ideas that are injurious. What's more, a third you exists—the "lyric you"[5]: he who observes, keeps watch, analyzes from afar, takes in data, then writes from a distance. In the end, all that matters is that all of you are bruised.

////

An NDN is the soul of a country. Racism, then, is a kind of moral death drive, an ethical desertion inflected on oneself.

////

The NDN condition: being in but not held by the present; belonging to a past that endures and a future that moves backward. The problem is that the present is in the air, is *now*, which is always an empty hand opening and closing inside us, like a heartbeat.

////

If nothing else, a sustained loneliness thrusts one into a moral position: to be emptiness animated or personified is to be a two-legged warning sign.

AN ALPHABET OF LONGING

ASYMMETRY

I pick myself up off the page + I throw myself at it again =
I throw myself at myself. [Repeat.]

Don't touch my skin, it is a text in the making.

I hoarded dirt in my ears; months later, I pulled out a summer
dress. When no one was looking, I ran it up a flagpole, so as to
be allegiant to something other than my captor.

A tree screams in the forest—forgive me, not a tree, but an
explosion of girls, an apocalypse of girls.

In an ecology of a clenched fist, sadness is at once the fist
and the fugitive air.

Love can make even the smallest of spaces feel too large. How?

BIOSOCIAL

I cough and it is a historical cough. I have a coughing fit and it,
as though a bellow, shocks those nearby into an alertness that
is historicist. My coughing activates a reading practice in those
cognizant of the anatomical debt borne by bodies like mine.
One way my doomedness manifests is in the sense that I need
to hoard a lifetime of living in just a few decades.

BLAME

Blame isn't a question just of emotion but also of the politics
of space. Concealment, hiding blame, is an architectural project,

a visualizing practice. Everywhere, Canadians are forgiven for a history they continue to stage in the theatres of everyday life. What is a citizenry but an audience that took a sledgehammer to the fourth wall of history, said *a "we" is a weapon?*

The architects of blame can be found in departments of political science and history everywhere. Also at literary festivals. At the podium of one, a white poet prefaced a poem of hers with a heavy declarative statement: *Shoot me now!* For a surreal second, I thought perhaps she was serious and that it was neither rhetorical nor a distasteful joke. (There are many for whom such a declaration is always in the air as an effect of the spoiled codes of race.) To be a poet one can't use language so recklessly, I argued to no one. *If you love me, you will shoot me now. Before the poem begins.* This is what I heard as a kind of refrain, repeated by the audience too. I nonetheless knew that those three words were a whirlwind of white speech, wrecked and reckless. People in and of themselves aren't poems. Remember this.

DESIRE

Once upon a time, time. This is desire's organizing principle, its political anthem. Desire runs in all directions: forward, backward, into the earth, toward the sky. If it could it would hurl our bodies onto the ground with the force of the history of human dissatisfaction. It would stamp us into our environments, amalgamating our interior and exterior lives (we rarely autonomously choose the latter), which is something we've all wanted at one point or another. (Richard Siken, in *War of the Foxes*: "A blurry landscape is useless.")[1] Desire, like writing, initiates a war waged against the "I," its permanency regime.

In desire's path we are a thread of smoke unspooling from a stranger's lips.

"Desire is no light thing," writes Anne Carson in *Autobiography of Red*.[2] Desire is heavy, dark, serious.

Desire is to time as the hunter is to the hunted, one might speculate. It seems to me, however, that desire is to time as the forest is to the hunter *and* the hunted. "The enormity of my desire disgusts me" (Siken).[3] An enormous desire is a climate whose logics elude anthropological explanation.

Desire is a present-tense verb whirling into the future tense.

Desire unfinishes us.

Desire unfurnishes us: we are houses out of which it empties the furniture such that we can be peopled again.

DISPOSABILITY

I'm a walking sacrifice zone. Immaterial, I'm a supposition of a person; a trial run that exposes mechanical error upon mechanical error.

When I write, it feels as though I'm clawing at a ceiling lined with dandelions. The spores and dirt shower onto me, their velocity diametrically opposed to my writer's block. I eat and eat until I'm more dandelion than anything else. The work of art festers inside me.

EMPTY BED

Suppose an empty bed were

   an expression of politics rather than a negation of it.

   a poem from the future.

   the scene of a riot.

   a painting without a focal point.

   evidence that love is a grey smudge on a map of the Americas.

FREEDOM

I want to hold freedom close, like a newborn baby.

   That is the wrong approach. You understand this too.

   Freedom isn't a sibling rivalry. Our survival isn't a matter of motherly love.

In the early hours of my political awakening, I felt that I *had* to do something about all the gay men who devoted themselves firstly to lust and not to freedom. There was an undercurrent of desperation here, as though my suffering were correlated with their pessimism. Their unnumbered days and weeks and months had become mine (see BLAME)

I couldn't fuck my way out of white supremacy. (One can accomplish the opposite, unfortunately.)

Men left their dirty worlds in my bed. They are always there, especially when the men aren't.

GENDER
When two bodies embrace they become a window. Gender is what's heard when wind touches glass. Remember: by the time sound reaches the flesh, innumerable bursts of light have already shot through us.

HOPE
The settler state ≠ the world.

LONELINESS
Loneliness: an echo; the skin rubbing up against another world, the resulting friction; a philosophical position; an aesthetics; a bludgeon made out of bones; a blurry face in an old photograph; a revolving door.

This is my non-definition.

LOVE
To a room of conference attendees, I said, "I'm an emotional person, so I read theory day in and day out."

Love is the act of ramming headfirst into the window of an "I." Some nights I release a deep, sharp breath so as to draw two stick figures drowning in a frozen lake. *You're so warm*, an ex-boyfriend would tell me, barely awake, a pale semi-colon shivering against my back.

The mode of writing I'm bound to is something like what Roland Barthes in *A Lover's Discourse* describes as "outbursts of language," which he attributes to the lover who is overrun with ideas, who is jammed in the aesthetic realm of fragmentation, struck by "aleatory circumstances."[4] Barthes attributes an immobility to this discursive state; it is destabilizing and all-consuming such that one can't move on, as though a word or an idea could keep us tethered to the ground. If I'm in love with neither another person (an Other) nor the world, what then is the object of my affection which wrenches me into the kind of rhetorical frenzy Barthes sketches out? The answer is obvious: I'm a lover of the prefigurative, the makeshift, the missing.

Confession: my lovelessness is a symptom of the settler's bastardized possibility.

NDN HOMO
NDN homo in a dead world.
NDN homo made of corrugated sensation.
NDN homo under the foot of history.
NDN homo an ethnographic spectacle.
NDN homo a mythology of desire.
NDN homo an erotic symbol.
NDN homo a postmodern slut.
NDN homo nothing but enigmatic traces of others (Butler).
NDN homo a brutal inheritance.
NDN homo glistens inside the smokescreen of liberal empathy.
NDN homo a cliché.
NDN homo an ongoing degradation.
NDN homo a poetic impulse.
NDN homo a tenant of the terrain of bad feeling.
NDN homo an architecture of emotion unto himself.
NDN homo a speculative historian.

NDN homo a post-structuralist suspicious of form.

NDN homo in a struggle with the appeal of always being in a struggle.

NDN homo a haunted house, a racially saturated visual field.

NDN homo fuckability.

NDN homo fugitivity.

NDN homo at the limits of political subjectivity.

NDN homo a corrosion of personhood.

NDN homo a sonic revolt from the future.

NDN homo a narrative door (Halberstam).

NDN homo in potentia.

NDN homo an optical illusion.

NDN homo a shape of a life, a philosophical gesture.

ONTOLOGY

I take residence in a dumpster locked inside a parking garage. There is no ontological difference between the dumpster and me. We are mimetically liminal, both purged of ethical matter. To be young and in love in a dumpster, in the constitutive outside of the present, is a manifestation of melancholia.

Do you know how mindless I've been about where I plant my feet? The manner in which I stand determines whether I'm a statue or a monument.

PESSIMISM

Somewhere a courtroom is painting an image of NDNs as a people outside the law, seizing us in the age-old position of the savage, the brute. I wonder how it is that we haven't simply become brutes and dug our teeth into the flesh of the country that has pursued us in bloodlust for centuries.

REFUSAL

If I refrain from writing, no one can misunderstand me (Kierkegaard inverted). The more practical option is to burn all the maps of the province of Alberta in nôhkom's front yard and inhale the smoke.

You can affix a price tag to anything—including a poem—to strip it of its treacherous affectivity.

There is no moneyed writing where I'm headed. The anecdotal is a hiding place. Join me.

Audra Simpson (Mohawk) taught us that it isn't lucidity of which we NDNs are envious. In fact, the settler's drive to coax us into an orthography of deficiency isn't the final nail in the coffin of pre-history. Our indecipherability turns out to be material for a commune of rebellion.

Better days are neither ahead nor behind us. We are stuck in a loop of pseudo days where what unites us isn't clock time but a dizzying drama of half-moments that refuse to aggregate into the outline of a lifestyle. There is a formlessness to our slanted existence. This is a cause for celebration.

RELUCTANCE

A poem isn't a coin-operated machine.

REVENGE

The purpose of NDN writing isn't to fatten the body of Common Sense, that rickety scarecrow.

None of your crying will unsick or unkill anyone.

Push this book out to sea. If you are forested, the river of your tears will do.

I'm ravenous for the future, but my longings are incompatible with the available versions of it. Bummer.

Angie Morrill, Eve Tuck, and the Super Futures Haunt Qollective: "This is a body made from all of the missing and gone faces. It is at once lovely and horrible and there are so many."[5] Some of us are barred from the terrain of attraction, our faces too ringed with caution tape.

I almost said I felt like a puzzle, but it is so unpoetic to be a puzzle! To be a puzzle is to be a carcass picked clean, and I'm supposed to do the picking.

The thing that makes men manly is that they force everyone to be witness to their vengeance. I want no part in this.

REZ FAG[6]
Can the Rez Fag speak?

The Rez Fag both is and isn't: how are we to undo the ideational deficit of melancholy?

Everywhere the Rez Fag is pulverized: at the kitchen table, at the Band Office, at faculties and departments of Native and Indigenous Studies.

To talk about the Rez Fag
you have to talk about circuitries of unbecoming
and to talk about circuitries of unbecoming
you have to talk about the ghosts in the machine of
relationality
and to talk about the ghosts in the machine of
relationality
you have to give up on the allure of self-sovereignty
and to give up on the allure of self-sovereignty
you have to destabilize the body as the sealed
container for political life.

STATISTICAL SUBJECTS
Enumeration is an exercise that banks on a cruel form of nostalgia.

STRANGER
A conversation between me and me:
What is a stranger? I ask.

(Silence that sounds like yesterday, like the end of a long season.)

Nothing, an outline of a life, a fill-in-the-blank puzzle, he answers. I push at his side.

So we're simply two nothings trashing against each other?

Not simply, he replies. *Metaphysically, a stranger leaves no mark, makes no noise. The trace of nothing is still nothing. Zero added to zero is zero.*

What if a stranger is a question mark unfurling inside the chest? The most pressing question, then: Who has posed you as a conundrum?

TERROR

Former Bank of Canada governor David Dodge, on the Trans Mountain pipeline: "There are some people that are going to die in protesting construction of this pipeline. We have to understand that."[7] There are killing fields where understanding blooms. Sometimes knowledge is a rope made of poison ivy. Why does anyone think it is more rope we need?

THEORY

I don't want to construct another ship made of poetry. My poems didn't float, so I didn't make it to shore.

I wanted you to look away as you ripped the wet pages from me. Instead, you wrote: *Run*. Sentences jutted from my mouth like laughter.

I asked to be a newspaper, finite and refutable information, but I was instead given a papery chest with which to instigate a new economy of pain.

My chest is so big it could be an ocean floor. Inside me, a cacophony of poets. "An embarrassment of poets."[8]

UTOPIA

Utopia isn't a feeling but rather the banished shape of an ur-feeling. It is in one valence submerged in an ethics of privacy.

Invisibilized, utopia is against a sovereignty of the senses.

In a more politically rousing valence, it is incommensurable with publicness, being instead an unownable thing that barks back at the interpellative shout of property.

In Muñoz's Cruising Utopia, utopia appears again and again as an insurgent force with which we smuggle ourselves into the future, with which we activate the ecstatic (a word Muñoz uses to speak to the convergence of past, present, and future).[9]

My project: A ricocheting "no" torpedoed at a world, a repudiation of a world in which NDN life is a fiction that leaves us wanting, caught red-handed, intoxicated on the promise of our impossible longevity. Also: a performance of a theory of nonsingularity and care that forgoes the melodrama of individuality.

It isn't that NDNs bear an essence that is somehow unhampered by social power. Have you taken note of the assaults of the many-headed beast of settler rage as of late? NDNs are moved—positioned and oriented—not in the direction of the dead future that state violence anticipates but instead toward a time and place gushing with all that this violence can't extinguish, which is our metaphysics of joy.

VOICE

I don't want my voice to be churned through a biopolitics of data collection that is the process of racialization. I won't take part in a performance of self that entraps me in a vicious circle of proof-making.

My field of study is NDN freedom. My theoretical stance is a desire for NDN freedom. My thesis statement: Joy is an at once minimalist and momentous facet of NDN life that widens the spaces of living thinned by structures of unfreedom.

I will spend the rest of my life enfleshing this argument. This catalog, then, doesn't and can't end.

ROBERT

May 2017. Our second date. Positioned, cautiously, a couple feet apart on the couch in my ever-shrinking four-hundred-square-foot apartment in downtown Edmonton, we are bowled over with laughter.

Moments before, I'd gone to the bathroom. I sat on the toilet to pee and fished my iPhone out of the pocket of my black super skinny jeans, which I bought in England, where retailers have yet to succumb to the masculinist renaissance of "slim fit." (Scrolling through tweets while my bladder emptied, it occurred to me that straight men my age likely don't partake in this form of multi-tasking. Standing to pee seems like a relic of a bygone era; nowadays we maximize excretory time. Yet another unanticipated confluence of the gay agenda and late capitalism.) Buzzing with glee, I fashioned this text message to one of my best friends: "MAJOR EMERGENCY! CALL 911!!! We ended up back at my apartment and I'm feeling very FRISKY!" Much to my alarm, this wasn't sent to its intended recipient, but to you, Robert. I flushed the toilet, washed my hands, and then quickly opened the bathroom door to say *GOTCHA*—my unimaginative attempt to smother the sense of embarrassment flowering in the pit of my stomach.

Grinning, you brush it off as a quirk of mine—and you're not wrong, I do silly shit like this all the time. Nonetheless I'm racked with nerves and struggle with basic motor skills; I spill water on myself when I lift the glass to my mouth. You don't notice, so I fill the quiet with a proposition: *Can I kiss you?*

Hours later, two orgasms later, we slow dance in my bedroom at two in the morning to the sound of nothing, to the acoustics of desire. In my head, Elton John's "Your Song" plays on repeat. Already, I wish to leave the old future out to dry in tomorrow's sun. What good is it now that I've tasted on your lips all the hope in the apartment? When you leave, so too does hope. I have wanted nothing more or less than this.

////

July 2017. Post-sex, fixed in the pale light of an overhead lamp, sprawled across my mattress on the floor, you are so motionless, Robert, it looks as though you're a painting ruled by sentiment. I hope you're possible of such grace, so that I too can be. We, two men of no aesthetic significance, engineered beauty from stolen time with our lumbering bodies. All my psyche can hold is the past, present, and future tense of the moment. I lie down beside you, the sheets rustling beneath us, as though we've made a forest floor of our yearnings. I want to live a whole human life in this bedroom of wet hands, where, for evenings at a time, the world starts and ends without celebration or remorse. What I know: We aren't running away. The eyes are too hungry for their own good. There is yellow of endless gradations—I want to see you tiptoe into all of them. Beside you, bound together in the same puny blaze, there is little to believe in besides the promise of our infinite luminosity. Dozing off, it occurs to me that if there is a corrective to the problem of my existential loneliness, it is this study of light.

I feel unhinged, as though I were adjusting to a new frequency of everyday life, to a new gravitational force—call this care. I drift toward an elsewhere or a nowhere; it's difficult to decipher, so I make a republic of longing out of you. I become a citizen of the negative space around you. With each date, after I ask you to be my boyfriend and you say yes, I inch closer and closer to a Not-I. I end up at the gate of a becoming-us, which is a non-place at best.

It is in the shoddy and unmappable world of a non-place that object lessons abound, especially those about the exhaustibility of hope, about how "exposure to otherness" is the condition of possibility for relationality as such.[1] I'm someone who worships at the altar of the post-structuralist notion that to be with others is to be undone by them, which is a state of being regularly intuited as love, "one of the few places," according to Lauren Berlant, "where people actually admit they want to become different."[2] To me, this means that in order to architect a livable world with someone, a loved one, with you, I have to undergo a process of self-abolition, to be in a position of existential risk.

As such, I empty myself into you—I have seen this everywhere on the reserve: bodies like invisible monuments. I spend hours beside myself in a loop of anxiety and depression that is against vitality—the antidote to which becomes the sparse texts you send throughout a long workday. Shortly into our new relationship, I decide, perhaps prematurely, that we're brimming with possibility. I watch YouTube videos for hours on end of weddings, gay and straight, marinating particularly in the nuptials, which are a part of an ever-compounding embargo on bad endings that is the hallmark of monogamous coupledom. I spend a lot of time thinking about bad endings. My hunger for you and with it the solidity of feeling that coupledom promises whirls inside me, non-stop, brash. Were you to press your ear to my chest, you would hear not a heartbeat, but a persistent growl, or what you might mistake for one.

What is it to enact care in a non-place? In her introduction to *Matters of Care: Speculative Ethics in More Than Human Worlds*, María Puig de la Bellacasa rescues care from the trap holes of a "moralistic feel-good attitude" and "warm pleasant affection" and emplaces it in "ambivalent terrains,"[3] where it's imbued with the power to rend the patterns of thinking of the present.

I want to refuse to "disentangle care from its messy worldliness."[4] Like Puig de la Bellacasa, I believe care is disruptive and world-bearing; it "can open to 'as well as possible' configurations" in a present that injures some more than others.[5] To care in a more feminist sense is to think outside of a singular life, and to do this is to participate in a process of self-making that exceeds the individual. With care, one grows a collective skin: "the fact of being touched by what we touch."[6] Care detonates that which precedes it; it pulls us outside our bodies and into that which one can't know in advance. We, however, are readied to blend into the unknowable.

/////

August 2017. A humid Saturday afternoon. You work unendingly until Friday evening, which is when you drive sixty minutes to make waste out of time with me for a few days. You arrive sexually aroused, so we ignore our emptied stomachs in the name of another type of emptiness, a non-sovereign one, an irreparable one. I burrow my face into your butt, my closeness to which drowns out the soundscape of downtown Edmonton. Suddenly I feel a small metal object tumble up or down my nose—direction is eschewed in this sexual configuration. I politely ask you to jump off of me, which is when I realize that one of the studs on my septum ring has come loose in the ebb and flow of anilingus. I excuse myself only to swallow the stud in the bathroom. When I return to bed we've both lost our hard-ons. Potentiality, I learn, can bloat and then burst at any given moment.

We laugh about this incident for the next handful of days. It briefly smoothes the rough patches of my suspicion that you aren't gambling with your sense of self in the ways I do. It gives me something to hold on to as evidence of a shared world that has a plural "you" as its axis.

The problem is that I love you. The problem is that I'm in love while bound at the ankles to a country.

Shortly thereafter, you ask me to break up with you. Desire is too unruly for someone like you; it is too tempting, too gratifying, to sext with a normatively attractive man on the other side of the world, for example. I can't drown out the chorus of anxieties about your past life and the what-could-be that awaits a world without me. If love is world-building, then heartbreak is an implosion. I block you on Facebook. Delete you on Snapchat. I begin the labor of sitting inside the silence that pulsates in your wake.

////

Late August 2017. After just two weeks apart we meet up at, of all places, a mall, where we both have Saturday night plans. You apologize profusely to me, tears welling in your eyes. I look into them as though they'll save us from what our hands are capable of. I accept your apology, believing that you are less wildfire than before. You tell me that you've ceased being able to determine what to do with yourself, which revealed to me that you hadn't yet mustered the courage to call grief by its ugly name. Back at my apartment, we sway from side to side backlit by the moon. I tell you I want to make love, not fuck. Cliché, yes, but it feels as close to prayer as I've been. When we kiss, I vibrate, as though a waterfall were rushing through me. My world had become so tiny you filled it entirely. Is that so wrong?

This is our last dance. Neither of us knows this.

////

November 2017. I'm re-reading a book of poems in which your name appears a number of times. Put off by how utterly mine I make this, I shelve the book. For me, "Robert" is not merely a name or a set of memories, but a sign system, an electric field of sorts that animates a way of life. I'm compelled by the shock of this encounter with an undead past to scavenge in the ditch of history. The loneliness is unforgiving, dispossessive. It occurs to me that I wish I had a picture of us hugging, for it was never simply an embrace, but a giving over of oneself to another.

/////

December 2017.

B: Hey! You've been on my mind lately. How're things?

R: Coincidentally, I'd also been thinking of you lately. Who knew a two-word question would prove so difficult to answer succinctly. I guess I've been OK, had to kind of re-plan my life in Canada after I left camp. Honestly, didn't think I would ever hear from you again and having a weird mix of anxiety and various other emotions as I type this (the fact it's 3 a.m. probably isn't helping lol).

[Later.]

B: I had a feeling that we'd at least chat again. For whatever reason, seems like loose ends were left untied—at least for me. Seems wild to me that you're living in central Alberta haha. How's that been? Fairly conservative there, eh?

R: Yeah, I didn't like how we left things. It felt wrong somehow. I'm glad you messaged me. This place is a pit lol. Full of casual racism and homophobia. Feeling very out of place. But I have my own place in a nice house which makes life somewhat bearable.

B: Someone once called that town the armpit of Alberta and I was like "mhmm, ya," though perhaps armpits deserve better than that sort of comparison haha.

R: Well we both know how you feel about armpits haha. I'm really glad you messaged me, btw. There have been a few times I wanted to but didn't really feel like I should.

B: Aw, well I'm glad I messaged too. What have you been meaning to say?

R: Well, happy birthday was one haha. But also I hated how things were left. I worried that you maybe thought I had done things while we were together that contributed to you needing space and cutting off contact. Also my profile on Scruff which tends to contain things just to get attention, which I now feel stupid about. I never thought we would go this long without talking.

B: Well, I had to cut off contact because I had such strong feelings for you, and I knew that seeing you on Facebook would upset me.

R: Yeah, I understood that. I guess I was just feeling shitty and sorry for myself—on brand for me lately. Do you feel like you're at a point where we could consider each other friends?

B: I mean, I still feel like you messed up something that could've been dope haha. I reached out thinking maybe you had reflected on that.

R: I have and I agree that's the case. I'm holding back a bit because I'm at work and don't want to appear visibly upset in front of customers.

B: Honestly, I still feel like I'd give you another chance, so IDK how that and friendship would mesh.

R: Fuck, I kind of wish you hadn't said that. Fucking up and breaking up showed me how much I cared for you, but I was sure you hated me so much that it didn't matter what I felt.

B: Gotta listen to your heart, Rob.

R: Something that I clearly need to spend a great deal of time working on.

B: So, what now?

R: I'm not sure. What's possible? Do you maybe want to talk after I finish work?

B: Yeah, I'd like that.

////

January 2018. I weather two dense hours as you drive to Edmonton. By "weather" I mean I did nothing; usually, I gnawed at the sun. This was our ritual. You worked this into the rhythm of us, and I conceded to you. Conceded: this is the word I use to describe the structure of feeling into which you had coaxed me. Slowly, I'm pouring myself into the floorboards of you. Soon, I will be an abandoned house, there will be nothing left of me but scaffolding. Lately, I can't help but nauseate on the vulgarities of our relationship: the two breakups, both of which were kindled by your world-risking craving for the rote of sexual attention that's the hallmark of hookup apps like Grindr and Scruff.

My anxiety calls up this moment from last summer: I heard you masturbating in the bathroom. My gut instinct was to be furious, as though you'd breached an unspoken social contract that any pleasure should be a collaborative project when we're in the same space. Around that time, however, you struggled to keep a hard-on when we fucked. Rather than read into this as a repudiation of me as an erotic being, I vowed instead to try harder to exude sexiness when with you, to demonstrate to you that I ached to be attuned to all your sexual motions.

////

January again. I dig through your cell phone and find what I was looking for, against myself: incriminating evidence. Soon you're stirred awake by a bout of food poisoning. I pretend I'm asleep. You vomit on and off for five hours. You fall back asleep at 7:30. I get up to begin my morning routine. I look at you as though you're an emptied thing, a non-object from which there is nothing to mine. This is what it is to be torn from a "thick mesh of relational obligation."[7] Again, I'm at once wordless and

worldless. This is a blow to subjectivity that follows the origi-
nary one care unleashes. One can anticipate the first ontological
explosion of falling in love. The second one is somewhere in
a land mine into which one can only ever trespass.

////

February 2018.

B: Hey Rob! I wanted to write to say I unfriended you (which
was rash, sorry). I've been reflecting on you and us lately—
probably all of the sad music I've been listening to and my two
weeks in the mountains, which compel one to turn inward haha.
I decided I should write to say thank you for what we did have,
rather than end on what went wrong. In classic "us" style, we
ended on a rough note, so, if you hadn't been my boyfriend, my
family wouldn't have been able to see me in love. I wouldn't have
known what it's like to want to put all that you can into someone else, like SERIOUSLY, romantically, shamelessly. I hope
you're well.

////

Both falling in love and falling out of love illuminate the deep
ambivalence of care about which Puig de la Bellacasa writes.
Care doesn't easily retrieve us from the fragilities of cohabita-
tion; it plunges us into a zone where everything shape-shifts,
where everything is a potential site of severance and constitu-
tion. A relationship as new and spastic as this one shows how
care makes one straddle the fence of bifurcated times and
places. In the aftermath, care promises nothing, but this doesn't
mean that we must put a restriction on it. Care is a disruptive
thing because it frees the analytic of the world from a state that
is overdetermined. And so, those of us who still want love in the

couple form dwell in the instabilities of caring for that which also has the power to undo us. But always, with care, we perform high-stakes processes of world-making—in the hope that, in our dying days, we might feel freer.

NOTES FROM AN ARCHIVE OF INJURIES

1. Dionne Brand (*The Blue Clerk*): "I walked into a paragraph a long time ago and never emerged from it."[1] Maybe this act of getting lost in the textual is a spur to life, to aliveness, for those who have been barred from, whose barring makes possible, the biosphere of Canadian Literature. Canadian Literature is a crime spree. How frequently can one redraw the outline of a body and still call it art? The police—which Frank Wilderson reminds us is both an institutional form and the corporeality of whiteness itself[2]—made an oversized archive of our injuries. I feel their fingers in the pages of me when I write.

2. The problem of sending out dispatches from a life as it is being realized is a problem of bioethics, broadly construed. Any dirt road out of the wilderness of my body is so ridden with potholes it is undrivable.

3. To write as though a punching bag requires a different kind of bad posture.

4. All my most volatile and consuming yearnings could be summarized as a desire for an unstructured life, one without an organizational system other than something like untidiness. I don't wish to be subject to the wrath of any clock, including the biological kind. (The clock of utopia is one I adhere to but adhering to the clock of utopia is akin to sleeping on a couch constructed from love poems, a fate I will always choose.) Writing disarrays the world around me. With writing, I'm authorized to rebel against the biopower of permanency.

5. If there is an "NDN experience" perhaps it is that of being written about. Audra Simpson: "To speak of indigeneity is to speak of colonialism and anthropology, as these are means through which Indigenous people have been known and sometimes are still known."[3] There exists a modality of anthropological inquiry practiced by Canadians from all walks of life by virtue of having been born into a story of confederation and dispossession. To nod to Brand's theory of black life and presence, to go outside the limits of one's own existence as a racialized subject (which is cramped and ever-shrinking) is to enter into "some public narrative," a narrative of progress, for example.[4] To write so as to peel sentences from one's skin, so that words fall flat onto the floor without the hope of resuscitation—this is the NDN writer's work. This usage of the English language at least matches the intensity with which words have been flung at us like grenades.

6. NDN literature: to treat language brutally while still writing beautifully.

7. Fred Moten and Stefano Harney: "The open song of the ones who are supposed to be silent."[5]

8. A dead animal overwhelms a highway the way moss does a forest floor. This is my unstable definition of poetry.

9. I have lived. (The most dishonest sentence I have written.)

10. In *Senses of the Subject*, Judith Butler asks a colossal question that tailgates me everywhere I go: "What does it mean to require what breaks you?"[6] She is curious about the indeterminacies of being in the world, how that which constitutes selfhood—being in concert with others—also has the power to loosen our grip on a shared reality. I've evoked this formulation in the past to understand the metaphysical thrust of queerness; in a late-capitalist world in which individuality is a fetish, a mass object of desire, a political anthem,

what remains queer about queerness is that it entices us to gamble with the "I" in the name of love, sex, friendship, art, and so forth. There is a twinned horizontality and verticality to queerness that pulls at the self in various directions. It is through this directionlessness, by offering ourselves to it, that we evade acclimatizing to or being seduced by the norms of social legibility and a subject position coded as the bearer of regular life (a dangerous duo). To write about oneself seems also to be an affair with breakage. To borrow Anne Boyer's phrase, there is a "range of textual annihilative desire[s]"[7] that make up a book, all of which are aimed at the writer by the writer. Some days, the act of writing isn't so much holding a mirror to oneself but to a future grave. When I write myself into the haunted house of Canada, the dark spins around me as though my body were yet another empty room it could get inside.

PLEASE KEEP LOVING:
REFLECTIONS ON UNLIVABILITY

Desirous of a beautiful life I get out of bed, but it's Monday and I'm in the throes of a genocide. I make a cup of coffee and pick up a poetry collection, both of which I attend to at my living room window; for a few minutes, I think of nothing besides coffee, poetry, and windows, which feels like a small rebellion. In the corner of my eye I see a banner I constructed many months ago that says no settlers / in the future. I'm not in the future. I'm in the present; this means I'm as lonely and as brief as a country.

When I open the pages of the book, I'm transported to an elsewhere unhinged from misery toward which I can run. I begin to distrust everyday life, which is a conduit for grief's traversals; at the very least, I'm inclined to waste away weeks and months inside the literature of radicals for whom the present is a mistake, a ruse, something to turn our backs on. If all we need is one overdetermined reason to suffer the mode of aliveness, perhaps art is mine. Perhaps if Billy-Ray Belcourt is a concept that shouts and dances and philosophizes I'll in the end have been scattered in thousands of pieces across the nation. Everywhere will be my graveyard. I'll have lived and died as that which is more than the sum of my body parts. What will matter isn't how many days I endured in the battleground of linear time, but what every fiber of me aspired to—something more than the gift of mortality, more than the rusty category of the individual who had meaning spewing from his ears, something only fully and fleetingly realized in the hands and mouths and chests of those whom I encountered as a ghostly mark on the page.

////

How silly that we measure the day by how much light fits inside it and not by the number of ordinary wounds the light lands on at any given second.

////

There's dizzying evidence of the unlivability of Canada wherever one looks. That NDN kids, NDN women and men, queer and trans NDNs, are all enticed by the freedom of non-existence is an ethical problem at the core of Canadian modernity. It's worth noting that "the world" isn't a passive noun, one given unto itself by way of common sense; rather, it's a unit of power, and as such it harbors the toxins of history. NDNs, those against whom the world swelled into an oversized, self-destructive one, are made disproportionately susceptible to an existential sort of poison, to being suspended on the barbed-wire fence between life and death. That we haven't sufficed in the project of making being in the world an arousing and joyous thing for all is a cause for alarm.

To begin to articulate what drives NDNs to kick-start a premature death, the conditions of which the state brews, we require a new grammar of living, one that foregrounds the fact of our utopian modes of being. I tried to do just this in a poem I axed from *This Wound Is a World* about the eleven residents of the Attawapiskat First Nation who attempted suicide on April 9, 2016. I sought to paint an image of contorted living in a pocket of the world that engenders exhaustion as a symptom of governmental neglect. To infuse the body of he who takes his own life with a complex form of agency was a herculean task I didn't want to risk botching. There had to be another way to go about this, without the room for mishap that verse pried open. This, then, is an experiment in writing in the direction of a time and place that doesn't produce suicide as a chronic condition, as a suitable response to trauma.

////

There's a way to talk about and represent suicide that's not pathologizing. The webseries *Feral* follows the frayed lives of a host of twenty-something queer artists in Memphis, Tennessee, and does just this. Through a non-linear, powerfully incoherent narrative style, *Feral* reveals bits and pieces of the doomed relationship of Billy (Jordan Nichols) and Carl (Ryan Masson). It's slowly made clear that Billy and Carl are in the thick of a mode of loving that is profound and world-shattering, so much so that it's difficult to think of them as separate people. Each short episode carefully elaborates the festering sense Carl has that to stay, to be in a body, to say yes to life, is too exhaustive an undertaking. Billy refuses to give up, to move on, to make love elsewhere; this is the sort of beauty in the face of existential deprivation that's especially useful now, in these dark times, in the fascist renaissance unfolding all over the West. Days before he takes his life, Carl whispers this to his boyfriend, who couldn't be away from him, couldn't let him go, *Please keep loving, Billy.*

This is an occasion not to romanticize suicide but to reflect on how to practice radical empathy for those who experience aliveness as a kind of ever-present death knell. *Feral* asks us to refuse to be entranced by easy fixes for the sicknesses of capitalist modernity, the corrective to which is an overthrowing of normal life. The webseries, in the end, posits love—queer, feminist—as what vitalizes the memory of the unjustly lost and functions as the foundation for a world that, like a benediction, is a promise of the glory of a dawning futurity.

////

I seek out a beauty that isn't subject to interruption, a beauty free of contestation. The kind that manifests as performances of social life and embodiment that run counter to the world. Beauty as a troubling of normality Beauty as an indictment of the status quo. Beauty as what it is to exist in the register of futurity.[1]

At a reading, another poet says my love of beauty is abundantly clear. To be compelled to write beautifully about unbeautiful matters is a minor miracle, but it's also to declare that the world has been poured onto me and that anyone within earshot has the power to wield a word like a match.

////

Nested at the mouth of the Attawapiskat River on James Bay in northern Ontario, the remote Cree community of Attawapiskat is a pressurized site for the convergence of forces that stomp suffering into the rut of statistical truth. In one sense, suicide emerges as a political response to structurally manufactured sorrow where joy has been shut out of everyday life for a long time. The manufactured sorrows include inadequate and improperly constructed housing, overcrowding, state mismanagement of funds, ecological harms, intergenerational trauma, and so on. It should be unsurprising to those of us who attend to the long elaboration of colonial violence from coast to coast to coast that these sites for bad feeling are all propagated by a decades-long governmental project to suppress NDN vitality. We might think of these environmental stressors as grim reaper—like, foul things that feed on the happiness of us, one by one, until something like the soul has been picked clean. What else would compel more than one hundred people at Attawapiskat—whose population is only 1549, according to the 2011 census—to try to end their lives between September 2015 and April 2016? I write today on the side of joy, to expand its geographical confines against the tentacular ways the state and its gruesome history extinguish possibility in the lives of NDNs.

What do we owe the machine of living, which gushes its venom at the innocent? By innocent, I don't mean those unscathed by politics, which is an impossible position to occupy. Purity is a misleading thing. With this troubled word—"innocence"—I want to nod to those in a brawl with the world as a consequence of what they signify in the arena of national sentiment. How any of us survive a world always against us, against what we signify and make imaginable, is a sociologically significant act. What I know is that it's unfair that NDNs are called on to make do in a world we neither wanted nor built ourselves. I have called this bind precarity. It's also the ground zero for suicidal ideation.

////

The Neskantaga First Nation in northern Ontario has been under what is essentially a permanent state of emergency since 2013, as compromised living conditions continue to govern life and death there. In April 2016, after the aforementioned suicide attempts on a single Saturday, the Attawapiskat First Nation declared a state of emergency too. Liberal Prime Minister Justin Trudeau called the "news from Attawapiskat" heartbreaking, and Charlie Angus, the region's Member of Parliament and New Democratic Party Indigenous affairs critic, called it a "rolling nightmare." This governmental speak, this action-less language, does little to ameliorate the conditions that elevate suicide to a state of emergency. "Emergency" is a key word here, for it indexes a set of circumstances that call for an immediate end to the "rolling nightmare." "Emergency" is a noun that yanks us from the normality of daily life, but its invocation also promises to grab us by the hand and lead us to safety. The addition of "state of" here is also important insofar as it butts up against "emergency"; it stretches the word out, which denotes its protracted nature, its velocity and scale. The emergency isn't one emergency but a pileup of emergencies. On the other hand, the state of emergency can be understood as a singular emergency; it is the emergency of Canadian history.

I wrote this poem in the wake of a suicide pact carried out by two girls, aged twelve, on the Wapekeka First Nation in January 2017, published in *This Wound Is a World*—perhaps another attempt to use poetry to get at a deeper understanding of why some NDNs choose death:

> in january 2017,
> two girls, 12, carried out a suicide pact
> on the wapekeka first nation.
> what is suicide
> but the act of opening up
> to the sky?
> what is suicide
> but wanting to live
> more than once?
> yesterday
> a cloud fell onto me
> and i never felt more at home.
> sometimes i cry in indian
> and it sounds like
> i am speaking
> in english.
> don't open your eyes.
> pretend that
> everything is a bird
> and no one is hungry
> for what they can't have

Set in the mood of the elegiac, I sought to reveal some of the aspirations that animate suicide: the feeling that life has stranded you; the making of heaven, of the sky, as an NDN world of sorts; the woe of being severed from your mother tongue; the existential hunger that drives men to do egregious things to women and girls and boys. "don't open your eyes," then, is an ethical call, a note of care and instruction, that has to do with the possibility of another way of looking, one that might illuminate a future in which the clouds aren't more hospitable to NDNs than Canada is.

////

A country is an argument against beauty.

Ocean Vuong: "I want to insist that our being alive is beautiful enough to be worthy of replication."[2] How to be alive outside the affective register of the state, inside something less structurally sound, where to be lonely isn't to ruinate?

Not every melancholic is buried in his longing. I want a song or a poem or a myth to drape over me like a fourth layer of skin. To be a gust of life, à la Roland Barthes, pirouetting throughout the world—how graceful!

////

The Cross Lake First Nation in Manitoba also declared a state of emergency, on March 9, 2016, in response to 140 suicide attempts in the preceding two weeks. An editorial in the *McGill Daily* argued that the so-called "suicide crisis" or "suicide epidemic" couldn't be resolved without accounting for the region's ecological harms and economic insecurity. NDN activists and scholars have similarly been quick to point out that the high incidence of suicide and suicidal ideation on reserves has everything to do with funding shortages for adequate and culturally safe mental health facilities, racism in urban centers that do offer services, and other forms of social and political violence. But Dr. Alex Wilson of the University of Saskatchewan also insisted that many of the youth from Cross Lake who attempted to or did take their lives were LGBTQ-identified and that this wasn't being factored into public discourse. Perhaps part of what overwhelms a more precise interrogation of the particularities of this NDN death drive is the way words such as "emergency," "crisis," and "epidemic" sensationalize rather than humanize those who exit the world. There's a poetics to be tapped into that pries apart these concepts, one that disappears the mist of signifiers so as to allow us to conceptualize suicide as of a piece with the long war on NDN life. To prevent premature death, we are all beholden to doing away with uses of haunted speech.

On March 10 of that year, the Native Youth Sexual Health Network, a grassroots organization by and for NDN youth that operates in the United States and Canada, and for whom I used to work, received an email from a family doctor stationed in northern Manitoba, pleading for help as he was worried that homophobia and transphobia weren't being taken up in the mental health crisis intervention strategies by the federal government and the band leaders. For many, the "suicide crisis" on reserves is a crisis of trans- and homophobia.

Suicide is routinely coated in negative affect, for it marks the loss of a life that could still be here. I, however, want to be able to talk about suicide as both devastating and as a kind of politically charged reaction to a world that makes living at the intersections of social loci untenable. Suicide prevention, then, can't simply be about keeping NDNs in the world if it remains saturated by that which dulls the sensation of aliveness for those who are queer and/or trans and/or two-spirit. History and its ongoingness drove us to a point in which abandoning the world elbowed its way to the front of the line of individual agency.

Suicide prevention thus needs to entail a radical remaking of the world.

In her beautiful and painful collection of songs and stories *Islands of Decolonial Love*, Leanne Betasamosake Simpson writes, "suicide's not something you do to other people, it's something you do for yourself."[3] Value judgments that smother suicide in shame extend the violence that stunted the lives of queer and trans NDN youth in the first place. If "suicide prevention" is the analytic we're going to attach to, then it needs to be about making new forms of collective NDN life, ones that don't cherry-pick ways of being over others. Reserves can be incubators of transphobia and homophobia as a symptom of the Christianizing project carried out by settlers for decades; that history, however, doesn't absolve NDNs of making use of a single-issue focus on race that ignores to a grievous degree the pain of the doubly and triply marginalized.

NDN youth, listen: to be lost isn't to be unhinged from the possibility of a good life. There are doorways everywhere, ones without locks, doors that swing open. There isn't only now and here. There is elsewhere and somewhere too. Speak against the coloniality of the world, against the rote of despair it causes, in an always-loudening chant. Please keep loving.

FATAL NAMING RITUALS

Sometime in 2011, at age fifteen or sixteen, I ordered Beatrice Mosionier's *In Search of April Raintree* to my childhood home in Joussard. My oldest sister, an undergraduate student at Grande Prairie Regional College at the time, had been assigned the book in a Native Studies course. I wanted a glimpse into the intellectual world of post-secondary education, to read and to be moved, irreparably and unsuspectedly. I wanted to tiptoe into the mise-en-scène of a novel, to let what I might witness illuminate a way of writing, a listening and looking practice that I had only known as the suspicion of something more radical, more energetic and enlivening, unrulier and more complicated than "Language Arts."

With *In Search of April Raintree* I found all of this. I found a book that was more than a book; Mosionier's story of the lives of two NDN girls who care for each other in contradistinction to the cruel "care" of the state, of social services, was a searing indictment of Canada. It was a critique of this country's inability to stop compounding the brutalities that NDNs are made to endure. *In Search of April Raintree* refused to torpedo NDNs into the gutters of misrepresentation. Mosionier took the work of description into her own hands, and because of this she refused to offer up a rhetoric that one might describe as simple. That is, Mosionier wrote in the mode of "truth-telling" to paint a picture of complicated and compromised living in the crosshairs of settler governance. In this way, she laid bare a way of storytelling that always returns us to the possibility of NDN life unhampered by a coloniality of the present. Fred Moten:

"Anybody who thinks that they can understand how terrible the terror has been, without understanding how beautiful the beauty has been against the grain of the terror, is wrong."[1] Each word of Mosionier's book, each pronoun and preposition, all of them, shake with a vitality that is in the name of NDN freedom and nothing less.

There is an art to spinning words so that they are always-already against the monotony of voice and for the polyphony of political speak. This is the terrain of NDN writing. It always has been and always will be.

////

Say "forgiveness." With a maw full of smoke, say "the aftermath of history." Hold our books in your slippery hands with the ever-loudening fact of their eschewal of a reading practice that makes a feast out of "a choreography of mangled bodies."[2] Mouth the word "enemy," but don't enunciate it, for it isn't a subject position worth keeping in the world. Living as we do in the charred remnants of a time during which the voices of NDNs were siphoned out of the theatres of culture and into the wastelands of law and order, you, a white and settler you, are beholden to a project of lessening the trauma of description.

Everywhere in the colonial archive there is a plethora of descriptions that seek to hold the position of the NDN in a state we could describe as against opacity, as against the right to be unseen and unseeable. Colonialism is in part a system of clarity in the visual sense: what we and our communities look like becomes the basis for a mythology of race that refuses us the freedom to define ourselves. We were and still are made to exist in a visual field in which we're barred from democratizing the felt knowledge of our dignity.[3] In *Mohawk Interruptus: Political Life Across the Borders of Settler States*, Audra Simpson traces the political beginnings of "the savage" to the earliest moments of contact at which settlers did the terrible and terror-making work of classification so as to acclimatize the NDN to an atmosphere of ideas they transported from Europe. Today, we hear the resonances of this fatal naming ritual repeated and made anew. There are ways of thickening words with meaning so as to injure, of making words into evidence of our injurability. Hurled with the right amount of intensity, words floor us. There are words that lay me flat on the floor of the world. One of these words is "simple."

Simplicity is a mode of being in the world available to those enmeshed in white structures of feeling. Simplicity is an affect that motors the cultural imaginary of whiteness, an interpretive strategy. Simplicity hides a flurry of forms of social and political violence that rip the lives of the marginalized from the freedom of a good life, from a life emptied of historically contingent turmoil. Simplicity belongs only to those who live and write unfettered by all that ravages the world. It's an emotional orientation that enables one to pick up a book and put down a carcass. Simplicity is a structural impossibility for NDNs who make life hampered by state-sanctioned oppression.

On June 5, 2018, *The Walrus* published a review of my Griffin Poetry Prize-winning debut book of poems, *This Wound Is a World*, "Billy-Ray Belcourt's Simple and Radical Poetry." The title alone steals breath from the bodies of those who are roped into the unlivable and racialized terrain of simplicity—it was later modified by axing "simple" after writers like Gwen Benaway wrote incisive threads on Twitter critiquing the profile. The reviewer made use of the rhetoric of simplicity: words like "plainspoken," "straightforward," and "unmistakable" pile up to architect a thesis about method in poetry that has at its heart a binary between indecipherability and simplicity. There is nothing fundamentally poisonous about "simplicity," but it can be bathed in a tradition of wordliness or perhaps "language-ness," to use a term I first heard used by Layli Long Soldier, that traps NDN writers in the slum of plainness. The reviewer quotes a review of Mosionier's *Raintree* in *Queen's Quarterly*: "[Mosionier] sets out to tell a story—her own story—in the plainest available language. Nothing else is needed."

This interpretive behavior is everywhere in literary history. A classic of NDN literature, Maria Campbell's *Halfbreed* was also cited as part of a so-called simplistic literature. However both *Halfbreed* and *In Search of April Raintree* get at the sorrow and love that proliferates in NDN social words by creating what theorist Dian Million, in her essay "Felt Theory: An Indigenous Feminist Approach to Affect and History," describes as a "new language for communities." Million cites both Mosionier's and Campbell's texts as ones that punctured through the sound barrier of Canadian historical ignorance to tell "politically unspeakable" stories. Indeed, it was recently revealed that a chunk of Campbell's book was edited out because it detailed sexual abuse at the hands of members of the Royal Canadian Mounted Police, which would have surely thrown into relief the chronic problem of police brutality against NDN women. The late twentieth century, Million tells us, produced "a profound literature of experience."[4] Still, those who look and install meaning in words with the force of a history of impoverished reading negate the profundity of our writing.

The meta-claim underneath this line of inquiry is what we might call a "racial fatalism": in other words, it's as though NDNs were so bogged down by history, by bodies that emerge from that history, that we can only write in a way that is "plain," that is "sparse," that is "simple." The reviewer turns to a liberal interpretative strategy that seeks to empower a "humanity narrative" that is in fact a trapdoor, worthless in the fight against the cannibalistic genre of the human inaugurated in the laboratories of the New World.[5] It isn't that we need to be welcomed into the wasteland of the human, to be made fit for the operations of violence that uphold it, but a remaking of the world, one that flowers freedom for those denied it as a symptom of the many-headed hydra that is white supremacist capitalist heteropatriarchy.

In narratives that hinge on proving our humanness, NDNs sit stilled in the role of the described. As the described, our words are pit against us. Having only at our arsenal words that self-destruct, we shoulder the burden once more of voicelessness. How cruel to have our critiques of the ways in which unlivable lives are manufactured everywhere in Canada heard as evidence of our ability to speak and nothing else!

////

"My story was maltreated." So begins Terese Marie Mailhot in her memoir *Heart Berries*. *Heart Berries* elaborates a theory of ethical living, of how we might tune our ears to hear the always-compounding ways that NDN women are denied care. It isn't just that we're called on to listen in a mode that might breach the smokescreen of liberal empathy (to testify), but also and more importantly to treat a story so as to read and act in the direction of the world it begets. So, it isn't that contemporary NDN writers are speaking in unison, as if in a chorus uttering the same things, all in the name of a singular avowal of that which impedes our flourishing. We are all caught up in the singularity of coloniality, but each book, each poem, each story *is* against the trauma of description, those ways of reading and listening that make vampires out of people, possessed by an insatiable hunger for a racialized simplicity that makes us into objects of study to be fed through the poorly oiled machines of analysis.

To tell a story of the possibility that swells up even where it is negated requires a sociological eye, an epistemological stand-point, that is born out of experience, of knowing what it is to be a map to everywhere and nowhere. What's more, to hear this story of compromised living, of joy against the odds, of the repeatability of a history that lives in the bodies of those who reap the spoils of colonialism, as something more than a "simple" account of a singular life, is to undergo a process of resubjectification, one that requires the abolition of the position of the enemy, the vampire, the one who describes, the settler. You need to read, to listen, and to write from someplace else, from another social locus, a less sovereign one, a less hungry one.

All my writing is against the poverty of simplicity. All my writing is against the trauma of description.

////

Today, the world is just beginning, so I pack light. I start and end with books by NDN writers. With Layli Long Soldier's *Whereas*, I "Mommy the edge"[6] between a painful history that isn't done with us and a still possible future that proliferates care. I call this edge the "eroding edge of pathos," which is where I jump from with Leanne Betasamosake Simpson's *This Accident of Being Lost*, an unruly and differently ruled text that welcomes us to "the space of the unspoken and the unwritten and the unsung."[7] It is here, Gwen Benaway tells us in *Passage*, that "passage is more than movement,"[8] is in excess of and prior to geographical change, is an ontological force as much as a creative-theoretical one. With these books I build a monument to futurity where we assemble another "congress / of selves," where we perform and enact everything we "long to know and hold" (Liz Howard in *Infinite Citizen of the Shaking Tent*).[9]

You aren't invited into our commune. We aren't yet at that point of hospitality. I won't tell you when the time has come.

"There isn't time here. There isn't ever time here. There is only *here* here, only land here."[10]

TO HANG OUR GRIEF UP TO DRY

Activists doused the statue of John A. Macdonald in Montreal in red paint a number of times in 2018. In so doing, they refused to live according to what Christina Sharpe calls "monumental time," in which history is motionless, dead, and outside the ethical tonalities of the present.[1] Instead, the activists insisted on a politics of accusation, throwing into focus the *longue durée* of state-sanctioned violence against NDNs in Canada. It isn't just that the blame was aimed at Macdonald and his ilk, but at time too, which carries with it the lethal resonances of a past that unmade NDN worlds with brutish accuracy. Time doesn't move as though a ghostly entity, but through the bodies of those endowed by history who seek to fix NDN life in a continuum of suffering. The red on Macdonald is red on the body politic, on Canada writ large.

Macdonald was, of course, an architect of genocide. An ethno-nationalist, his stint as Canada's first prime minister unleashed famine in the prairies (to make way for westward expansion), inaugurated the time-altering residential school system, and saw ruthless retaliation to NDN resistance (i.e., the hanging of Louis Riel for his part in the North-West Rebellion of 1885).[2] We are thus in the interval between his murderous past and a rotting settler state in the twenty-first century where there is an ongoing crisis of NDN death both social and physical. We haven't had time to hang our grief up to dry, for the mourning is never-ending and the erosion and interrogation of NDN livability is built into Canadian political life. Much of what followed Macdonald's age was a kind of extension and reimagining of his intimacy with brutality. We, NDNs, are given over to that brutal intimacy, against our will, as abstraction and ideality, not as ourselves, never fully material, never allowed to inhabit our messy materiality. Such is the fate of NDNs, the slow violence of being made to live as ideas do. One need not look too far to glimpse the carelessness with which others treat concepts (that free thinking careers into cruelty is a hallmark of racial capitalist modernity). What the statues of Macdonald do in opposition, perhaps, to the progenitors of trauma worship is bring out into the open the afterlives of dispossession and capture, their grim futurity. We can't look away. The blood is there, before us. Each day, it spills anew.

////

January 29, 2018.

Word reaches me that jury selection in the high-profile Gerald Stanley trial in Battleford, Saskatchewan, was carried out by way of a surgical exploitation of race-based loopholes in Canadian law. One by one, each potential juror with NDN features or an NDN cultural disposition was shown to be too biased or too implicated in the case to deliver justice (which, again, is blind according to an old Western legal fiction, so this apportioning of NDNs on the other side of law and order isn't unprecedented). "Shown" here indicates the performative power of the law—to bring about that which it names—and thus the insufficiency of NDN speech to mark another kind of advocacy on behalf of those whose killings are thoroughly politicized. Here's what the *Globe and Mail* reported from the courtroom: "Each time a person who appeared to be Indigenous took his or her turn, a single word emanated from the defence bench: challenge. The potential juror then walked slowly back to his or . her seat. Whether male or female, young or old, the potential jurors who looked Indigenous were blocked."[3] What resulted was an all-white jury, an end that demonstrated to the Boushie family and to those watching from their homes that what was to be scrutinized wasn't truth but the social conditions by which NDNs were to live and die. The courtroom in Battleford, like courtrooms nationwide, was a laboratory of sorts, an over-wrought zone of memorialization and colonial governmentality, yet another realm of confrontation in the long history of the catastrophization of NDN life and bodies.

////

February 2, 2018.

Hazlitt publishes Anthony Oliveira's long-form essay "Death in the Village."[4] News has recently come to light outside of the whisper network of Toronto's Gay Village that a serial killer has been targeting gay men via dating apps like Grindr. Oliveira beautifully and painfully accounts for the unbearable tragedy of losing a loved one without either a trace of his body or an answer to the question of his disappearance. Death, no matter how much it decorates our lives and this planet, regardless of the vast territory it stakes out in all of us, is always a badlands, a devastated and devastating environment in which no one wants to linger. Bruce McArthur's killing spree evinced the exhaustibil-ity of liberal correctives to state-sanctioned homophobia (that human rights wins didn't extinguish the proximity of queers to death), but also and significantly the ongoing indifference of the police and other institutional bodies to the plight of queers made susceptible to harm in ways that don't catalyze public rage or concern. Oliveira notes that police withheld from declar-ing a serial killer was on the loose and thus couldn't avow that queer men—many of color—were going missing under similar circumstances in Toronto. Trauma, made unspeakable in pub-lic, consumes, whittling a life down to the bare bones of emo-tionality: paranoia and a survival instinct. Made to endure too long in paranoia, the survival instinct glitches. "Survival" itself is an eddying concept: what is survival when the psyche is an unlocked door?

I'm quick to identify with the victims (who were much more than victims, unjustly reduced to that flat form of subjectivity by McArthur and the media). I have spent most of my adult life engaging in anonymous sex with men I met on dating apps. Men whose names I didn't know. Men whose faces I didn't fully see. Men who seemed to have given up on care, whose touch wasn't touch per se but something sharper, something heavier. Men I met in hotel rooms and darkened vehicles. Dozens of men, innumerable now that I've not labored to keep the memories of them alive. There have been hookups I've abruptly left out of a sense of impending danger, ones I've counted myself lucky to have escaped. Queer men know what lurks inside dead eyes and bowed heads. What happened in Toronto in McArthur's apartment, how the police poorly managed the case—this all refracted out into the world and thus into the bodies and minds of queer men of color everywhere in Canada. I felt as though I was a part of an endangered species. I still do. This is how I've learned kinship with my kind: danger finds us, on our knees, sweaty with want.

What makes a livable sexual life? Where does grief go when it is barred from institutions of justice? What do we do with our surplus rage and fear?

////

February 9, 2018.

I'm reading to a book club in Edmonton when the verdict comes down in the Stanley trial. Acquitted. Found not guilty of all charges. It took an all-white jury just thirteen hours to decide that Stanley was a free man, that Colten's killing was neither accidental nor premeditated but necessitated. The room compresses around me. Those still unable to process what this means look at me with heavy and wet eyes. Out of the duty that comes with the role of the public intellectual, I comment on how the verdict reminds us that we need poetry to counter the world of that courtroom, the logic that NDNs are dispensable in the face of property, capital, and democracy. That what poetry intimates is resistance to and a shelter from the killing machines and grim reapers who preside over much of the prairies. Perhaps, I suggest, poetry can caress the truth that the courtroom left to die. That we've congregated here under the presumption of mutual care and in the interest of a type of writing that punctures the solitude of a singular existence radically opens us up to joy, I tell them. There are words I can't speak, however. They line the walls of my chest, pulling me downward, compounding the earth's cruel appetite.

I drive absent-mindedly to my apartment, not needing to be alert to the road out of habit. I sit in my vehicle in the parking lot for thirty minutes, sobbing. The sobs come from a cavernous place inside me in which it is easy to get lost. There is a cavern of this sort inside all NDNs. Some of us reside there because we've stopped looking for an exit.

There's the quick, untimely death that Colten met, then there's the slow life and death that NDNs like me weather—we'll all know what it is to exist with the night sky underneath us. This is our Canadian tradition. The acquittal, the panic in the jurors (reported on social media by those in the courtroom), the insatiable hunger for NDN suffering in the prairies—all of this emerged from a centuries-old white imagination that has matured into a heartless beast.

On the one hand, poetry did nothing to prevent Colten's death or the subsequent and dizzying display of juridical violence in Battleford. On the other hand, poetry made room for me to grieve. A river of longing flowed through me. I feel its frenzied waters right now.

NDNs everywhere in this country, particularly those in my generation, have been indelibly altered by this ruling. I wonder: How will we ever look white people in the eyes and not periodically see our mangled bodies? This isn't hyperbole. We have Canadian citizenship, of course, and as citizens we will remember how to participate in the world, but we are still the hunted. The hunted speak of joy, and joy beckons the hunted.

////

This history of violence appears here, choreographed, because it hovers above me like—like what? A crow? An abandoned house? The sky? It reckoned with me in an existential manner. I felt doomed, so much so that objects and activities lost their aura of attraction. I didn't yearn for anything but privacy, because it is an embarrassment to be a wound in public.

When I think of an instance when a violence entangled categories of identity tighter with grief, I think of June 12, 2016. In the early hours of that day, Omar Mateen entered a gay nightclub called Pulse in Orlando, Florida, with an assault rifle and a pistol, shooting and killing forty-nine patrons and wounding fifty-three others. Later that day CNN reported that according to authorities the Orlando shooting was "the deadliest mass shooting in the United States" and "the nation's worst terror attack since 9/11" (this "deadliest" has since been used to describe the Las Vegas shooting). Partly in response to the impoverished, imperialist optic with which American media and politicians interpreted the shooting, Jack Halberstam noted in a blog post titled "Who Are 'We' After Orlando?" that this killing was "highly specific," for those gunned down by Mateen were at Pulse on "Latin night."[5] In an essay offered as a tribute to those killed at Pulse, novelist Justin Torres uses phrases like "every shade of brown" and "if you're lucky, they'll play some Latin cheese" to foreground the demography of Pulse on June 12: mostly Latin queers, some undocumented immigrants, many from places like Puerto Rico, a US colony "drown[ing] in debt."[6]

There was a two-fold sort of negation of queer-of-color life here: firstly, the dead were called up as subjects of American empire, as grievable life only insofar as their geographic location annihilated all other markers of identity; secondly, the shooting was fundamentally racialized and queered, in that Mateen corrupted a place of brown queer congregation, of brown queer sociality and aesthetics. If, as then president Barack Obama put it, we need to take shelter under an "us" to become "resolute against terrorists," if the families torn apart by Mateen "could be our families," then the interpellating call of this "us" and this "our" couldn't be answered by those killed on the dance floor of Pulse, those who were always-already banned from the territory of American futurity. Their lives couldn't be and weren't grieved by way of the sign of the nation. This called for another kind of politics of mourning, one that could account for the intersectional thrust of much homo- and transphobic violence: the "dangerous nexus" of race, gender, sexuality, and class, to use Kalaniopua Young's language.[7] If statist and popular discourse can't mitigate our differential vulnerability to premature death, then it won't propagate our grievability.

In the hours and days and weeks that impossibly and cruelly followed the Orlando shooting, I bore an acute sense of alienation, to my body and to the world. Tears welled in my eyes without a visible trigger. A queer co-worker and I vented about how fragile and violable our spaces of communion felt, especially in a province like Alberta in which homo- and transphobia are still underneath the sensibilities of average joes everywhere. Everything was dimmed, except the ever-solidifying threat that plagues queers of color in the Americas. Wherever there is a disavowal of something like brown queer joy, though, there is also its undefeatable excess.

This undefeatable excess is what I understand to be the poetic drive. Christopher Soto, a self-described "queer latinx punk poet," penned a beautiful poem called "All the Dead Boys Look Like Me" that articulates a method of thinking about Pulse that ruptures the optic of terror that deracialized and desexualized the deaths in Orlando. "All the Dead Boys Look Like Me" registers an affective structure that US government officials like Obama couldn't, an "embodied cultural surplus," to use Muñoz's language.[8] In it, Soto writes: "Yesterday, I saw myself die again. Fifty times I died in Orlando."[9] Here Soto confesses that for people like him, living on felt impossible in the wake of the Orlando shooting, that people like him are stuck in an interminable grief, that they're ontological misfits made to live, love, and dance near death. For Soto, those killed in Pulse had erected "cathedrals," cathedrals others mistook for cemeteries. There would be no proper living while brown and queer. The Orlando shooting was a heartbreaking reminder that the world isn't for queers of color, that "the whole world" wasn't ours "for the choosing."[10] In a video posted on YouTube mere hours after the Orlando shooting, Soto recited a poem by Ocean Vuong called "Someday I'll Love Ocean Vuong," first published on May 4, 2015, in *The New Yorker*. Fighting through tears, Soto breathes new meaning into the stanza: "Don't be afraid, the gunfire / is only the sound of people / trying to live a little longer / and failing. / Ocean. Ocean, / get up" ("and failing" is Soto's addition).[11] Importantly, "and failing" barely leaves Soto's lips, for it is now encrypted with a shattered queer life-world, transporting us across time and space to the dance floor of Pulse in Mateen's aftermath. In both poems, Soto seeks to enact a form of critical affect that might keep brown queer joy in the world, in a state that can't be attacked by those who seek to do so. At the end of "All the Dead Boys Look Like Me," Soto writes: "Yesterday, my father called. I heard him cry for only the second time in my life / He sounded like he loved me. It's something

I am rarely able to hear. / And I hope, if anything, his sound is what my body remembers first." This sound is the sound of a world-to-come imbued with brown queer possibility.

Vuong and Soto write not away from but into traumas mundane and spectacular. By installing the poem with an elegiac force that refutes pacification, that pairs grief and rage, they actualize a style of writing that is against doom—"Ocean. Ocean, / get up"—and one that is bent on illuminating the art of living on in the midst of an illogical and all-too-logical terror—"He sounded like he loved me." To write is to live on. The page rescues us from a longing for finality. Grief doesn't wholly assail our imaginations. The creative drive, the artistic impulse, is above all a thunderous yes to life.

////

What is it to account for freedom events, for enactments of liberatory desire, in a time mediated by signifiers of doom such as these? To be alert to freedom and doom is what I make of my job as a writer. It is my job because I'm aware of the conditional and thus refutable nature of both facets of social life. We can understand doom as the ways in which the knowledge of one's killability sits in the air, menacingly, and how that brutal information is renewed by quotidian and spectacular acts of violence in daily life. Freedom makes breathing easier; it begets an atmosphere governed by joy, not oppression. Freedom is a measure of breathability. A writer, then, is also the public's barometer of terror and freedom.

What does freedom demand? An old question, but one that requires ongoing renewal. My understanding of freedom's demands come to me by way of Foucault (we have to insist on our right to be free) and Muñoz and Dionne Brand and Leanne Betasamosake Simpson, thinkers who have all in their own ways refused the statist machinations that inhibit joy and possibility for queer and racialized peoples in the Americas and elsewhere. Simpson, for example, teaches us that woven into Nishnaabeg language and philosophy is a normative theory that instructs her people how to "dance through their lives with joy."[12] I'm reminded that freedom is itself a poetics, in that it seeks to reschematize time, space, and feeling in the direction of a future driven by an ethics of care, a relational practice of joy-making that is all of ours to enact.

Thankfully, Brand has provided us with mantras for political life in this anti-earth, cruelty-loving age of white dominance: "they hate our freedom,"[13] so "only freedom matters."[14]

They hate our freedom, so only freedom matters.

What determines our lives as NDNs and/or queers are pain and trauma, love and hope. Death looms at all scales, individual to planetary. But there is also an ecology of creativity, one indivisible from our futurity. In the face of an antagonistic relation to the past, let us start anew in the haven of a world in the image of our radical art.

ACKNOWLEDGMENTS

Stephanie, my agent, whose ambition and belief in my art are endlessly empowering.

Keavy, my doctoral supervisor, who had eyes on iterations of some of the ideas presented herein, who made my time in graduate school significantly more livable.

Maura, my dear friend, who listened to me bemoan the difficulties of writing on far too many occasions, who always laughs at my jokes.

Eric and Eliza, the team at Two Dollar Radio, who have granted this book another kind of life in the U.S.

NOTES

Preface: A Letter to Nôhkom

[1] Warsan Shire, *Teaching My Mother How to Give Birth* (London: flipped eye, 2011).

[2] José Esteban Muñoz, *Cruising Utopia: The Then and There of Queer Futurity* (New York: New York University Press, 2009), 73.

Introduction: A Short Theoretical Note

[1] According to cultural theorist Ann Cvetkovich, political depression emerges from the realization "that customary forms of political response, including direct action and critical analysis, are no longer working either to change the world or to make us feel better." See her *Depression: A Public Feeling* (Durham: Duke University Press, 2012).

[2] Christina Sharpe, *In the Wake: On Blackness and Being* (Durham: Duke University Press, 2016), 109. Sharpe is, of course, writing about the "breathtaking spaces" that emerge within the weather of anti-blackness.

An NDN Boyhood

[1] Sheila Heti, *Motherhood* (Toronto: Knopf, 2018), 124.

[2] The afterlife of history emerges of course from Saidiya Hartman's crucial "the afterlife of slavery."

[3] The "outrun" metaphor inspired by Terese Marie Mailhot's *Heart Berries: A Memoir* (Toronto: Doubleday Canada, 2018), 3: "We sometimes outrun ourselves."

[4] This is a line from my first book, *This Wound Is a World* (Calgary: Frontenac House, 2017).

[5] Ibid.

[6] Cited in Dylan Robinson, "Intergenerational Sense, Intergenerational Responsibility," in *Arts of Engagement. Taking Aesthetic Action In and Beyond the Truth and Reconciliation Commission of Canada*, ed. Dylan Robinson and Keavy Martin (Waterloo: Wilfrid Laurier University Press, 2016), 43.

[7] DukeWomenStudies, "2013 Feminist Theory Workshop Keynote Speaker José Esteban Muñoz," *YouTube*, May 8, 2013, https://www.youtube.com/watch?v=huGN866GnZE.

A History of My Brief Body

[1] "We Speak About Violence: Abdellah Taïa and Édouard Louis in Conversation," *Paris Review*, July 2, 2018, https://www.theparisreview.org/blog/2018/07/02/we-speak-about-violence-abdellah-taia-and-edouard-louis-in-conversation/.

[2] Recycled from "Duplex (The Future's a Fist)" in my poetry collection *NDN Coping Mechanisms: Notes from the Field* (Toronto: House of Anansi Press, 2019).

[3] Lee Edelman, *No Future: Queer Theory and the Death Drive* (Durham: Duke University Press, 2004), 5.

[4] Indebted to language in Mailhot, *Heart Berries*, 34: "It seems innate that I am fucked up."

Futuromania

[1] Lisa Robertson, *Cinema of the Present* (Toronto: Coach House Books, 2014), 5.

[2] Judith Butler, *Precarious Life: The Powers of Mourning and Violence* (London: Verso, 2004), 18.

[3] Dionne Brand, *Ossuaries* (Toronto: McClelland & Stewart, 2010), 84.

[4] Maggie Nelson, *Something Bright, Then Holes* (New York: Soft Skull, 2018), 24.

[5] Muñoz, *Cruising Utopia*, 49.

[6] See Hieu Minh Nguyen's "It's important that I mention, I truly wanted to be beautiful / for her." From "Changeling," in his *Not Here* (Minneapolis: Coffee House Press, 2018), 55.

Gay: 8 Scenes

[1] Archive on Demand, "Poetry Reading: Ocean Vuong," *YouTube*, March 29, 2017, https://www.youtube.com/watch?v=ZiVvQvvIPY4.

[2] Ocean Vuong, *Night Sky with Exit Wounds* (Port Townsend: Copper Canyon Press, 2016), 61.

[3] Eve Kosofsky Sedgwick, *A Dialogue on Love* (Boston, Beacon Press, 1999), 45.

[4] Mailhot, *Heart Berries*, 60.

[5] Belcourt, *This Wound Is a World*, 21.

[6] A modification of Dionne Brand's "sitting in the room with history." *A Map to the Door of No Return: Notes to Belonging* (Toronto: Vintage Canada, 2001), 25.

[7] Lisa Duggan, "The New Homonormativity: The Sexual Politics of Neoliberalism," in *Materializing Democracy*, ed. Russ Castronovo et al. (Durham: Duke University Press, 2002), 189.

[8] Judith Butler, "Critically Queer," *GLQ: A Journal of Lesbian and Gay Studies* vol. 1 (London: Gordon & Breach Science Publishers, 1993), 19.

[9] Maggie Nelson, *Bluets* (Seattle and New York: Wave Books, 2009), 15.

Loneliness in the Age of Grindr

[1] Nelson, *Bluets*, 15.

² Han Kang, *The White Book*, tr. Deborah Smith (London: Portobello Books, 2015), 10.

³ Jill Stauffer, *Ethical Loneliness: The Injustice of Not Being Heard* (New York: Columbia University Press, 2015), 1.

⁴ This is a nod to a poem in *This Wound Is a World* called "Ode to Northern Alberta."

Fragments from a Half-Existence

¹ Elizabeth Bishop, "One Art," in Muñoz, *Cruising Utopia*, 70.

² Leo Bersani, *Is the Rectum a Grave? And Other Essays* (Chicago: University of Chicago Press, 2010), 3.

³ Kang, *The White Book*, 77.

⁴ Bhanu Kapil, *Ban en Banlieue* (Brooklyn: Nightboat Books, 2015), 61.

⁵ After writing this vignette, I came across a reference to the "lyric u" in jos charles's *safe spaces* (Boise: Ashata Press, 2016), 15.

An Alphabet of Longing

¹ Richard Siken, *War of the Foxes* (Port Townsend: Copper Canyon Press, 2015), 7.

² Anne Carson, *Autobiography of Red* (London: Jonathan Cape, 1999), 133.

³ Siken, *War of the Foxes*, 8.

⁴ Roland Barthes, *A Lover's Discourse: Fragments*, tr. Richard Howard (New York: Hill and Wang, 2010), 3.

⁵ Angie Morrill, Eve Tuck, and the Super Futures Haunt Qollective's "Before Dispossession, or Surviving It," *Liminalities: A Journal of Performance Studies*, Vol. 12, No. 1 (2016), http://liminalities. net/12-1/dispossession.pdf.

⁶ This section is in response to an image of Demian DinéYazhí's by the same name.

[7] I first heard this quote in Dionne Brand's lecture upon the conferral of her honorary doctorate at the University of Toronto.

[8] Vahni Capildeo, *Venus as a Bear* (Manchester: Carcanet Press, 2018), 14.

[9] Muñoz, *Cruising Utopia*, 189: "Utopia in this book has been about an insistence on something else, something better, something dawning."

Robert

[1] Judith Butler, *Senses of the Subject* (New York: Fordham University Press, 2015), 16.

[2] Heather Davis and Paige Sarlin, "No One is Sovereign in Love: A Conversation Between Lauren Berlant and Michael Hardt," *No More Potlucks* (blog), Issue 18: amour, Nov/Dec 2011, http://nomorepotlucks.org/site/no-one-is-sovereign-in-love-a-conversation-between-lauren-berlant-and-michael-hardt/.

[3] María Puig de la Bellacasa, *Matters of Care: Speculative Ethics in More Than Human Worlds* (Minneapolis: University of Minnesota Press, 2017), 2, 5.

[4] Ibid., 10.

[5] Ibid., 12.

[6] Ibid., 20.

[7] Ibid.

Notes from an Archive of Injuries

[1] Dionne Brand, *The Blue Clerk: Ars Poetica in 59 Versos* (Toronto: McClelland & Stewart, 2018), 136.

[2] Frank B. Wilderson, III, "The Prison Slave as Hegemony's (Silent) Scandal," Ill Will Editions, June 2015, https://illwilleditions.noblogs.org/files/2015/09/Wilderson-Prison-slave-READ.pdf.

³ Audra Simpson, "On Ethnographic Refusal: Indigeneity, 'Voice' and Colonial Citizenship," *Junctures* No. 9, December 9, 2007, http://pages.ucsd.edu/~rfrank/class_web/ES-270/SimpsonJunctures9.pdf.

⁴ Graham Foundation, "Dionne Brand: The Shape of Language," *YouTube*, July 20, 2018, https://www.youtube.com/watch?v=r_HdOZIFEl0&t=1733s.

⁵ Fred Moten and Stefano Harney, *The Undercommons: Fugitive Planning and Black Study* (Brooklyn: Autonomedia, 2013), 51.

⁶ Butler, *Senses of the Subject*, 9

⁷ Anne Boyer, *A Handbook of Disappointed Fate* (Brooklyn: Ugly Duckling Presse, 2018), 57.

Please Keep Loving: Reflections on Unlivability

¹ In conversation with Saidiya Hartman's reflections on beauty: "Beauty… is a way of creating possibility in the space of enclosure": *Wayward Lives, Beautiful Experiments: Intimate Histories of Social Upheaval* (London: Serpent's Tail, 2019), 33.

² Ocean Vuong, *On Earth We're Briefly Gorgeous* (New York: Penguin Press, 2019), 139.

³ Leanne Betasamosake Simpson, *Islands of Decolonial Love* (Winnipeg: Arbeiter Ring Publishing, 2013), 81.

Fatal Naming Rituals

¹ Duke Franklin Humanities Institute, "The Black Outdoors: Fred Moten & Saidiya Hartman at Duke University," *YouTube*, October 5, 2016, https://www.youtube.com/watch?v=t_tUZ6dybrc&t=4620s.

² From *This Wound Is a World*.

3 "Felt knowledge" is a concept that Dian Million uses to signal ways of thinking that emerge from the context of emotional experience. See *Therapeutic Nations: Healing in an Age of Indigenous Human Rights* (Tucson: University of Arizona Press, 2014).

4 Dian Million, "Felt Theory: An Indigenous Feminist Approach to Affect and History," *Wičazo Ša Review* 24, no. 2 (2009).

5 To follow this line of inquiry, see the work of Black studies scholars like Sylvia Wynters, Katherine McKittrick, and Christina Sharpe.

6 Layli Long Soldier, *Whereas* (Minneapolis: Graywolf Press, 2017), 48.

7 Leanne Betasamosake Simpson, *This Accident of Being Lost* (Toronto: House of Anansi Press, 2017), 35, 11.

8 Gwen Benaway, *Passage* (Neyaashiinigmiing: Kegedonce Press, 2016), 10.

9 Liz Howard, *Infinite Citizen of the Shaking Tent* (Toronto: McClelland & Stewart, 2015), 16.

10 Morrill, Tuck, and the Super Futures Haunt Qollective's "Before Dispossession, or Surviving It."

To Hang Our Grief Up to Dry

1 Sharpe, *In the Wake*, 62.

2 Canadian Press, "Montreal's John A. Macdonald statue vandalized by activists," *Montreal Gazette*, Updated: December 24, 2018, https://montrealgazette.com/news/local-news/montreal-the-moment/montreals-john-a-macdonald-statue-spray-painted-by-activists.

3 Joe Friesen, "Family upset as jury selected for Colten Boushie trial," *Globe and Mail*, Jan. 29, 2018, https://www.theglobeandmail.com/news/national/familys-hopes-dashed-as-majority-white-jury-selected-for-boushie-murder-trial/article37784480/.

4 Anthony Oliveira, "Death in the Village," *Hazlitt*, February 2, 2018, https://hazlitt.net/longreads/death-village.

[5] Jack Halberstam, "Who Are 'We' After Orlando?" *Bully Bloggers*, June 22, 2016, https://bullybloggers.wordpress.com/2016/06/22/who-are-we-after-orlando-by-jack-halberstam/.

[6] Justin Torres, "In praise of Latin Night at the Queer Club," June 13, 2016, https://www.washingtonpost.com/opinions/in-praise-of-latin-night-at-the-queer-club/2016/06/13/e841867e-317b-11e6-95c0-2a6873031302_story.html.

[7] Tom Boellstorff, Mauro Cabral, Micha Cárdenas, Trystan Cotten, Eric A. Stanley, Kalaniopua Young, and Aren Z. Aizura, "Decolonizing Transgender: A Roundtable Discussion," *TSQ: Transgender Studies Quarterly* 1, no. 3 (2014), 428.

[8] Muñoz, *Cruising Utopia*, 161.

[9] Christopher Soto, "All the Dead Boys Look Like Me," *Literary Hub*, June 15, 2016, http://lithub.com/all-the-dead-boys-look-like-me/.

[10] Ibid.

[11] Christopher Soto, "Someday I'll Love Ocean Vuong," *YouTube*, Jun. 12, 2016, https://www.youtube.com/watch?v=PvEXIL4wplY.

[12] Leanne Betasamosake Simpson, *As We Have Always Done: Indigenous Freedom through Radical Resurgence* (Minneapolis: University of Minnesota Press, 2017), 8.

[13] Dionne Brand, *Inventory* (Toronto: McClelland & Stewart, 2006), 27.

[14] Brand, *The Blue Clerk*, 227.

Two Dollar Radio
Books too loud to Ignore

ALSO AVAILABLE Here are some other titles you might want to dig into.

WHITEOUT CONDITIONS NOVEL BY **TARIQ SHAH**

← *"Whiteout Conditions* is both disorienting and visceral, hilarious and heartbreaking." —Michael Welch, *Chicago Review of Books*

IN THE DEPTHS OF A BRUTAL Midwest winter, Ant rides with Vince through the falling snow to Ray's funeral, an event that has been accruing a sense of consequence. With a poet's sensibility, Shah navigates the murky responsibilities of adulthood, grief, toxic masculinity, and the tragedy of revenge in this haunting Midwestern noir.

VIRTUOSO NOVEL BY **YELENA MOSKOVICH**

← "A bold feminist novel." —*Times Literary Supplement*

← "Told through multiple unique, compelling voices, the book's time and action are layered, with possibilities and paths forming rhythmic, syncopated interludes that emphasize that history is now."
— Letitia Montgomery-Rodgers, *Foreword Reviews, starred review*

WITH A DISTINCTIVE PROSE FLAIR and spellbinding vision, a story of love, loss, and self-discovery that heralds Yelena Moskovich as a brilliant and one-of-a-kind visionary.

SOME OF US ARE VERY HUNGRY NOW
ESSAYS BY **ANDRE PERRY**

← "A complete, deep, satisfying read." —Gabino Iglesias, NPR

ANDRE PERRY'S DEBUT COLLECTION of personal essays travels from Washington DC to Iowa City to Hong Kong in search of both individual and national identity while displaying tenderness and a disarming honesty.

SAVAGE GODS MEMOIR BY **PAUL KINGSNORTH**

← "Like all the best books, [*Savage Gods* is] a wail sent up from the heart of one of the intractable problems of the human condition: real change comes only from crisis, and crisis always involves loss... There are few writers as raw or brave on the page. Savage Gods is an important book."
—Ellie Robins, *Los Angeles Review of Books*

SAVAGE GODS ASKS, can words ever paint the truth of the world—or are they part of the great lie which is killing it?

THE BOOK OF X NOVEL BY **SARAH ROSE ETTER**

⇢ A Best Book of 2019 —*Vulture*

← "Etter brilliantly, viciously lays bare what it means to be a woman in the world, what it means to hurt, to need, to want, so much it consumes everything." —Roxane Gay

A SURREAL EXPLORATION OF ONE WOMAN'S LIFE and death against a landscape of meat, office desks, and bad men.

Thank you for supporting independent culture!

Books to read!

Now available at **TWODOLLARRADIO.com** or your favorite bookseller.

TRIANGULUM NOVEL BY **MASANDE NTSHANGA**

← "Magnificently disorienting and meticulously constructed, *Triangulum* couples an urgent subtext with an unceasing sense of mystery. This is a thought-provoking dream of a novel, situated within thought-provoking contexts both fictional and historical." —Tobias Carroll, Tor.com

AN AMBITIOUS, OFTEN PHILOSOPHICAL AND GENRE-BENDING NOVEL that covers a period of over 40 years in South Africa's recent past and near future.

THE WORD FOR WOMAN IS WILDERNESS
NOVEL BY **ABI ANDREWS**

← "Unlike any published work I have read, in ways that are beguiling, audacious…" —Sarah Moss, *The Guardian*

THIS IS A NEW KIND OF NATURE WRITING — one that crosses fiction with science writing and puts gender politics at the center of the landscape.

AWAY! AWAY! NOVEL BY **JANA BEŇOVÁ**
TRANSLATED BY **JANET LIVINGSTONE**

⇢ **Winner of the European Union Prize for Literature**

← "Beňová's short, fast novels are a revolution against normality."
—Austrian Broadcasting Corporation, ORF

WITH MAGNETIC, SPARKLING PROSE, Beňová delivers a lively mosaic that ruminates on human relationships, our greatest fears and desires.

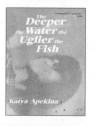

THE DEEPER THE WATER THE UGLIER THE FISH NOVEL BY **KATYA APEKINA**

⇢ **2018 *Los Angeles Times* Book Prize Finalist**

← "Brilliantly structured… refreshingly original, and the writing is nothing short of gorgeous. It's a stunningly accomplished book." —Michael Schaub, NPR

POWERFULLY CAPTURES THE QUIET TORMENT of two sisters craving the attention of a parent they can't, and shouldn't, have to themselves.

THE BLURRY YEARS NOVEL BY **ELEANOR KRISEMAN**

← "Kriseman's is a new voice to celebrate."
—*Publishers Weekly*

THE BLURRY YEARS IS A POWERFUL and unorthodox coming-of-age story from an assured new literary voice, featuring a stirringly twisted mother-daughter relationship, set against the sleazy, vividly-drawn backdrop of late-seventies and early-eighties Florida.